CONTENTS

INTRODUCTION

The $2 Trillion Mistake   1

How Traditional School Design Fails Our Kids

CHAPTER 1

"Reading" School Buildings   25

A Visual Literacy Primer

CHAPTER 2

A Welcoming Message   45

Entries and Common Areas

CHAPTER 3

Capturing More Space for Learning   61

Reconfiguring Classrooms and Hallways

CHAPTER 4

Integrated Learning Areas   83

Labs, Studios, and Do-It-Yourself Spaces

CHAPTER 5

Making Room for Collaboration   105

Professional Space for Teachers

CHAPTER 6

Putting People and Ideas Together   115

The Changing Role of the School Library

CHAPTER 7

Beyond the Classroom Window   129

Bringing Learning Outdoors

CHAPTER 8

From Cafeterias to Cafés   145

Celebrating Community

CONCLUSION

Putting Theory into Practice   159

Where Should Schools Begin?

APPENDIX A

Educational Effectiveness Survey   175

Elementary School Facilities

APPENDIX B

Educational Effectiveness Survey   179

Middle and High School Facilities

Notes   185

Acknowledgments   197

About the Author   199

Index   201

The $2 Trillion Mistake

How Traditional School Design Fails Our Kids

THE UNITED STATES has over $2 trillion of net worth tied up in its school facilities, making it the country's single largest educational investment.[1] A substantial portion of this investment is now at risk because of age and lack of adequate maintenance. The average age of schools in most districts across the nation is between thirty and fifty years. In the United States alone, on top of increasing routine maintenance expenses that total many hundreds of millions of dollars, over $12 billion is spent annually to modernize, add to, or build new schools.[2] Communities across the nation are scrambling to find funds simply to keep buildings operational. At least some of these funds could be spent redesigning classrooms and schools to accommodate student-centered learning.

Traditional school buildings fall far short when evaluated against the goals of student-centered learning. That is not surprising, because older school buildings were not designed to facilitate modern methods of teaching and learning. In fact, an older school building actually prevents the delivery of a true twenty-first-century education. This book will show how well-designed school buildings can be a catalyst for pedagogical change.[3] It will also provide educators with practical and cost-effective strategies to transform buildings so that education itself can be transformed.

The disconnect between what educators want to do and what their learning environment will allow them to do is a real problem for schools and school districts because the built infrastructure almost always represents their biggest investment. Not only that, but school districts also have to make huge financial commitments continuously to maintain a physical plant that is in conflict with their learning goals. Ironically, the more money a school district puts into an aging plant, the more invested it inadvertently becomes to the traditional educational model the plant dictates. This book will help school and district leaders align spending on their physical infrastructure with learning goals essential to students' success in the twenty-first century. Such alignment eliminates the false dichotomy between spending on infrastructure and spending on learning.

So what do our school buildings tell us about American education? The vast majority of them are designed as "cells and bells."[4] Students occupy cells called classrooms until the bell rings, and then they move on to another cell. This model has been prevalent for well over one hundred years but came into its own during the height of the industrial revolution, with the birth of Taylorism. Taylorism, named after industrial engineer Frederick Taylor, was about increasing efficiency through large-scale assembly-line manufacturing. Taylorism reduced skilled crafts into fragmented jobs in order to minimize skill level requirements and learning time for individuals on the assembly line. Workers were given a set task with a set result to repeat before the product moved on to the next set task, and their wages were determined by a "payment-by-result" system.[5] The school system, represented most visibly by the buildings in which students are housed, was designed similarly, as the planning of set tasks with set results was predetermined without student involvement. This education model worked well as long as it was preparing students to work in a manufacturing-based economy. In the school's equivalent of the factory, buildings are primarily designed for a teacher-centered model of education where adults "deliver" a curriculum to a passive audience of students usually via lectures.

Think about school buildings as the hardware within which the software of education runs. Like any piece of hardware, every school building also has limitations on what kinds of software it can run. The question we must ask ourselves is this: Do we design new software—the future of education—around the limitations posed by our existing hardware—school buildings? Or do we design a twenty-first-century education model according to what we think is best for students and then figure out how the buildings can be designed or renovated to accommodate this model?

On the face of it, most would argue that school buildings should not dictate how we educate our children—that "construction should not drive instruction." Indeed, most educators who oversee the renovation of existing schools and the construction of new schools probably believe that they are designing schools for the twenty-first century. This book will show how far off base that belief actually is. The reality is that almost all the schools that have been built or renovated over the past ten years or are on the drawing boards today are cells-and-bells schools—a design that makes them educationally obsolete on the day they open. Each school that we renovate or build today extends a defunct model of education for at least thirty years or more. This obsolescence is a huge problem for the United States.

If it is so obvious that we are sitting on trillions of dollars' worth of obsolete hardware and intentionally adding to that on a daily basis, then why don't we start upgrading our hardware so that it can run the software that we want it to run? This is a classic chicken-and-egg problem. We are stuck in a vicious cycle where obsolete school buildings perpetuate an obsolete educational model that, in turn, spawns additional obsolete school buildings.

If one were judging the quality of American education on the basis of the school buildings alone, it would be difficult not to imagine David Warlick's worst-case scenario: "The worst-case scenario is that ten years from now we're still graduating kids who are perfectly prepared for the 1950's."[6]

TWO VIEWS OF EDUCATION

There are, in fact, two prevailing views about education, teacher-centered learning and student-centered learning, and these two views have existed on parallel tracks for over a hundred years. Each approach to education calls for a different kind of school design.

Teacher-Centered Learning

This is the predominant method of education practiced across the United States. Throughout the history of public education, teacher-centered learning has been the dominant method employed by schools.[7] This model assumes that for students to learn effectively they must be continuously directed by a teacher. This view of education maintains that schooling's main purpose is to teach students a predetermined quantity of material—mostly contained in textbooks. The more material the students know, the more educated they are. Students are tested often to measure

FIGURE I.1   Teacher-Centered Learning

the extent to which they have learned the textbook-based material. Students start school knowing very little—they are empty vessels waiting to be filled. The expectation is that successful teacher-centered schools will fill them with information, knowledge, and skills by the time their education is done. Under this model, the teacher is responsible for ensuring that all students gain the same fundamental and essential knowledge regardless of their different abilities. Evidence shows us that this is very difficult to do—particularly in classrooms where there is a great diversity in student competence and aptitude. It is nearly impossible for one adult to constantly supervise twenty to thirty students while ensuring that each of them receives a personalized education.

Student-Centered Learning

Student-centered learning is a philosophy of education that centers on the student as an active participant in learning. Under this paradigm, every student in school is a worker and the teacher becomes a facilitator. The term *student-centered learning* can be viewed as an umbrella term encompassing several well-known teaching and learning practices, including project-based learning, personalized learning, and social-emotional learning. Student-centered learning allows the students to direct their learning, maximize their own personal potential, and develop the skills to

FIGURE I.2 Student-Centered Learning

apply theoretical knowledge to solve real-life problems—in physical settings suitable for this kind of applied learning.

Such learning is not a new idea. The progressive education movement that brought student-centered learning to schools is actually a late-nineteenth-century invention. The writings of prominent educational theorists like John Dewey, Jean Piaget, Lev Vygotsky, and Maria Montessori greatly influenced the movement through the twentieth century.[8]

The movement has gathered steam over the past two decades for two reasons. First is the increasing recognition, backed by research, that the knowledge and competencies for success in the twenty-first century are vastly different than those of the twentieth century. Harvard economists Claudia Goldin and Lawrence Katz discuss in their 2008 book, *The Race Between Education and Technology,* how education is failing to keep up with technology-driven skills demands of today's labor market. They also point out the growing income and achievement gap between college graduates, as only some of them leave with the necessary higher-level thinking skills needed for good jobs in today's economy.[9]

Second, research continues to solidify the argument that students learn better when they are personally and actively engaged in learning.[10] Research tells us that the student-centered model is more effective for deep understanding (as opposed to rote memorization) because it connects the learner with a wider range of experiences than just listening.[11] While student-centered learning is naturally effective in providing a diversity of activities, its real value lies in its ability to be personalized for each student.

This book accepts the perspective that learning is a reciprocal process between the learner, the facilitator, the pedagogical practices, the social climate, and the physical environment.[12] In a well-designed school, the reciprocity between learning and the learning environment would remain current and ongoing over the years. Unfortunately, traditional school buildings, no matter how well they were designed to serve educational needs on the day they opened, tend to become obsolete over time as technology advances and teaching and learning needs change.

In contrast, throughout this book, I have referred to the idea of a *learning building*— where an agile, active learner is supported within an agile, active social and physical learning environment. The learning building connotes both a building that supports student learning in a cutting-edge way (a building for learning) and a building that can be adapted to meet students' and teachers' needs as those needs evolve (the building itself "learns"). The idea of the learning building is explored further in this book.

A BRIEF HISTORY OF SCHOOL DESIGN

The United States introduced compulsory schooling between 1852 and 1917. Before that time, schools were almost all very small operations in churches or homes, and formal education excluded all but the rich and some of the very poor, who were to be "improved" in church-run schools. With the introduction of compulsory schooling came a need to efficiently manage many more students.

The schooling model adopted by most rural communities was the one-room schoolhouse. The quality of individual schoolhouses and the amenities they provided varied widely, depending on economic conditions. Usually one teacher would be responsible for teaching a group of elementary school children. Due to space constraints, multiage groupings were necessary. Depending on their age and capability, students were also given various assignments to do to keep the schoolhouse operating. School was usually open from 9 a.m. to 4 p.m., with two fifteen-minute recesses and a one-hour break for lunch. In addition to the educational function, the building served the community in another way: "The school house was the center and focus for thousands of rural communities, hamlets and small towns. Often, town meetings and picnics were also held there."[13]

FIGURE I.3   The Upper Boxelder One Room Schoolhouse was originally built thirty-five miles northwest of Fort Collins, Colorado. The school was built in 1905 and cost $290. It closed in 1951 and was relocated to Fort Collins Museum & Discovery Science Center.

Academically, the purpose of the compulsory education movement was to create literate and numerate citizens, but the one-room schoolhouse (perhaps inadvertently) also taught many social, emotional, and life skills in a way that its larger, urban counterparts were unable to do. Ironically, students were more likely to achieve many of the skills and competencies needed to succeed and thrive in the twenty-first century in the one-room schoolhouse than in the factory-model schools that followed and continue to this day.

The roots of the compulsory education movement can be traced to the Prussian movement, begun one hundred years ago and intended to train the lower classes to be obedient soldiers and serfs, rather than, necessarily, scholars. To this end, and as the one-room schoolhouse was no longer adequate to serve larger populations of students, modern schools began to resemble factories for teaching, with every student given the same desk, chair, and orientation to the lecturer at the front of the room. Perhaps unsurprisingly, this change happened at around the same time that the Fordist concept of mass manufacturing became more widespread. Like widgets on conveyor belts being ferried past factory workers to be prepared for sale, students in the original modern school were prepared in different subject areas by different teachers in different rooms, which were connected by long corridors. In the elementary school, this progression happened over a yearly rather than a daily basis, as students progressed up through the building to a different room each year.

Movements against this trend have bubbled along since its inception, when the ideas of some of the great thinkers in education at that time, such as Maria Montessori, were clearly quite incompatible with rooms comprising rows of desks and chairs. The open-classrooms movement of the 1970s was one such trend against the conveyor-belt style of schooling. Yet the factory-model school has persisted by default and continues to be adopted across the nation despite very little research to endorse it as a good way to educate children for today and tomorrow.

Nowhere is the Taylor industrial model of "efficiency" more studiously followed than in the way school buildings are designed and set up. Under the Taylor model, management made all the important decisions and workers were simply told what to do and when to do it.[14] Since the goal of factories was to produce identical widgets, it made no sense to have individual workers do things differently from each other. Education also was seen as a method by which all students would learn the same things at the same time from the same teacher. Individual differences between students should not preclude them from being trained to acquire the low-level information and skills that schools were expected to deliver. A system that worked for factories was expected to be just as successful for education, and indeed, one can argue, as Virginia Heffernan does, that schools were quite good in providing a level of basic training that was sufficient for graduating seniors to work competently in a factory: "The industrial-era classroom, as a training ground for future factory workers, was retooled to teach tasks, obedience, hierarchy and schedules."[15]

Arguments raging in the education community about the best way to educate students (teacher centered versus student centered) did not spawn a corresponding movement to change how school buildings were designed. This is not to say that there has been no innovation in school design—only that such innovations are limited to less than 1 percent of all schools in the United States.[16] The dominance of the factory model school was challenged for a very short period, during the mid-1970s, when attempts to connect the design of schools to a student-centered approach to

FIGURE I.4 Canning Vale College in Perth, Western Australia, is based on an open plan design. It is different from the failed open-classroom schools of the 1970s in that the design is not one large, open space. Rather, the design creates discrete zones for various activities while still retaining the agility of an open plan to provide for various-sized groups of students and interdisciplinary work.

education began in earnest. However, this movement that led to the creation of what came to be widely known as *open-classroom schools* flared briefly and ended in disrepute. A review of the open-classroom movement can help us understand how the movement has prevented subsequent efforts to update school design to current standards.

Open-Classroom Schools

The legacy of the open-classroom movement, and the myths surrounding its failure, has stalled progress in the school building arena for thirty-five years or more. Open-classroom schools (sometimes referred to as *schools without walls*) originated in the United Kingdom and migrated to the United States in the late 1960s. They were based on the belief that students will do better if they are removed from the constraints of the boxed-in classroom. The idea was to move from a teacher-centered model of education to a multiage, student-centered model. Physically, it involved the removal of classroom walls so that a team of teachers could work together in a large, open space where different-sized groups of up to two hundred students could be brought together according to interest and ability. Open-classroom schools were very popular through the mid-1970s.

In practice, most of the open-classroom schools did not live up to their promise, for two key reasons. The most evident reason was that the philosophy the schools embodied was not practiced by teachers, who sought to create the equivalent of traditional classrooms using room dividers and furniture. The second reason for the abandonment of the open classrooms is that they got caught up in the general backlash against the experimental culture of the 1960s. Schools designed for open classrooms soon had walls put up, and the movement to create open-classroom schools was completely dead before the end of the 1970s.

A third reason why open-classroom schools failed is less well known but is probably the most significant reason for their disappearance. This has to do with the design of open-classroom schools. Few people understand that the design of these schools had some fundamental flaws. Under the best of circumstances, putting one hundred to two hundred young children in one large, open area is an extremely risky proposition.[17] Without quiet zones, restorative areas, enclosed spaces for smaller groupings and focused work, handpicked furniture, and acoustic treatments that would be essential for the different activity zones to work as desired, the open-classroom design is almost certain to fail. Looking back at the actual design of these schools, it is evident that none of the above elements of design were actually put into place and so it is not surprising that open-classroom schools were dismissed as a fad.

Despite their ultimate demise, open-classroom schools remain disproportionately influential today in decisions about school design. Their legacy lives on mostly in the form of the myth that any change from a traditional classroom-based model of education represents a return to the failed open-classroom movement.

The damage caused by this myth is that it stands in the way of designing an effective student-centered alternative to the current cells-and-bells model. Even though student-centered learning starts with the same premise as did the open classrooms—that each student is unique and deserves a personalized education—today's architectural response obviously has to be very different from the failed open-classroom design.

Today, a new imperative for redesigning schools is the increasing role that technology is playing in education. Technology is enabling dramatic changes in the workplace, and analogous changes should also be occurring in learning environments but are forestalled by rigid design that has its roots in the failed open-classrooms movement. So how do schools and school districts reopen the discussion of school design to move it away from an obsolete factory model to one that is (yes) more open? And how do they do this without running into the wall of opposition put up by the opponents of open-classroom education?

First, it is important for any school leader who is interested in ushering in change to become an expert in the whole open-classrooms movement. The leader needs to understand why open classrooms came into being and the history and politics behind their demise. The best write-up on open classrooms is by Larry Cuban, who presents a complete and balanced perspective on the subject.[18]

To put it bluntly, our country now has over $2 trillion worth of dysfunctional architecture that is ill suited to educate children in the twenty-first century. This book will provide very specific strategies to reverse this dysfunction so that our existing school facilities can remain viable and effective for many years to come.

DESIGN FOR EDUCATION

School buildings need to be designed from the ground up to support four essential design principles (see the sidebar "The Four Design Principles for Schools"). They need to be welcoming, be versatile, support various learning activities, and send positive messages about activity and behavior. This approach is very different from how most schools are currently designed, where function and not quality leads the way. That means schools' designs are evaluated on the ability of individual spaces to meet their defined function and not much else. Classrooms are considered good if they can accommodate a certain number of students, cafeterias are successful if they can turn around a certain number of students within a prescribed amount of time, labs are effective if they have the required equipment needed to deliver the curriculum, and so on. The design principles that I address go beyond basic functionality and get to fundamental questions about the quality of a school building defined by its ability to meet basic human needs of dignity, social well-being, and emotional development. Of course, by fulfilling these needs, we also create a climate in which students can grow and thrive educationally.

SIX EDUCATIONAL STRATEGIES THAT THE DESIGN PRINCIPLES SHOULD SUPPORT

The four design principles identified in this chapter support the following six educational strategies: student-centered learning; teacher collaboration; positive school climate; technology integration; flexible scheduling; and connection to the environment, community, and global network.

Student-Centered Learning

The main purpose of student-centered learning (discussed earlier in this chapter) is to make learning more personalized for every student. It is also intended to encourage students to become more self-directed and improve their social and emotional development while building a foundation for acquiring the skills and competencies needed in the twenty-first century. From a teaching perspective, practices would change quite significantly from a teacher-centered model so that the teacher is a guide and facilitator rather than the director of learning and the purveyor of all knowledge.

THE FOUR DESIGN PRINCIPLES FOR SCHOOLS

Four criteria are imperative in any successful school design:

- *Be welcoming (safe, nurturing, encouraging good citizenship):* How students behave in school has a lot to do with the hidden messages that the building sends. The designer has great influence in setting up the environment so that it feels welcoming.
- *Be versatile (agile and personalized):* A school building has to be agile—which, as the I discuss throughout the book, is more complicated than just creating flexible spaces. Personalization refers to providing environments that meet the different needs and learning styles of different students.
- *Support varying and specific learning activities (multiple learning settings):* Some areas of the school should be designed to promote a variety of learning activities—for example, the learning commons. Other areas should be designed to support specific activities—for example, the black-box theater.
- *Send positive messages (about identity and behavior):* The importance of creating a positive school climate cannot be overemphasized. A school facility's design will have a big impact on efforts to create a positive climate.

Teacher Collaboration

Traditional school architecture promotes teacher isolation by limiting each teacher to his or her "egg-crate" classroom. Such a physical arrangement makes team teaching difficult and limits opportunities to build social relationships.[19] A collaborative teaching environment helps reduce burnout, improves teaching practices, and promotes a shared responsibility.[20] Just as traditional egg-crate architecture supports isolation, space can also be designed to support a professional learning community for teachers. Teacher collaboration benefits not only teachers but also students. According to a 2011 Stanford study, when teachers collaborate more, students do better.[21] This study concluded that "social capital," which is built when teachers have more opportunities to work closely with their peers, is more effective than "human capital," which is the professional development offered by outside experts. Moreover, teacher collaboration allows schools to offer more interdisciplinary projects, team teaching, and block scheduling—all of which support twenty-first-century education goals.[22]

Positive School Climate

There are many ways in which schools are trying to improve school climate. Several organizations have been formed to improve school climate, because of growing awareness that how students feel about school directly affects how they perform in school. One organization promoting positive school climate, the National School Climate Center, defines a positive school climate as "a safe, supportive environment that nurtures social and emotional, ethical, and academic skills."[23]

Positive school climate has been linked to social-emotional learning programs. This type of learning involves the instruction, development, and practice of skills to manage and express feelings, resolve conflict, and make responsible decisions. The premise of social-emotional learning programs is that in order for students to become collaborative learners, they must first learn how to communicate and work together effectively. A meta-analysis by Durlak and colleagues showed that social and emotional learning programs provide many benefits to students. The programs improve students' behavior toward each other and teachers, improve students' attitudes about themselves and school, and decrease emotional stress and depression. With their improved social skills and ability to identify and manage their emotions, students reach greater academic achievement.[24]

This book argues that school building design can be a very significant (and often overlooked) force in creating a positive school climate.[25] For example, it is possible to break down the anonymity of large school buildings through the creation of physical learning communities where smaller groups of students and teachers share a common space or community. Here all the adults know all the students by name and all the students also know each other personally. Under this system, bullying and other antisocial behaviors are reduced and conditions for improved academic outcomes are also created. Other ways that school design can create a positive school climate include properly designing and placing toilets, designing entries that are welcoming, creating areas for more social interaction, making food and beverages more easily available and convenient to access from social spaces, and providing more spaces to display student work.

Technology Integration

Nowhere is the influence of "disruptive innovation" more evident than in the technological arena.[26] Companies like Tower Records, Kodak, Polaroid, and Blockbuster were literally put out of business by new technologies that made their products and services obsolete. Information, the staple of schools, is now freely available at the touch of a button or the click of a mouse, and yet schools have resisted the urge to reinvent themselves so that they can serve today's children and today's education needs.

Few would disagree that digital literacy is essential for success, even survival, in today's world. Digital literacy is the overarching term for a wide array of skills, including the use of various popular software products for word processing, spreadsheets, presentations, photo and video editing, desktop publishing, and so on. It also includes Internet research, the creation of and participation in online blogs and discussion forums, Internet gaming (some of which has significant educational value), tweeting, and programming. Digitally literate students will also be able to connect with special-interest groups whose members are dispersed throughout the world, take online courses to improve specific areas of interest and passion, and start online businesses for trading or selling products and services. Perhaps the most exciting learning opportunity offered by technology is represented by the *maker movement*, which gives budding designers all the tools they need to realize their creative visions using open-source electronic platforms like the Arduino, laser cutters, and 3-D printers, whose costs continue to drop every day. In their book, *Invent to Learn*, Gary Stager and Sylvia Libow Martinez argue that "this 'maker movement' overlaps with the natural inclinations of children and the power of learning by doing."[27]

School buildings, with their sterile computer labs, highly restricted access to the Internet, limited availability of mobile computing devices, and marginal use of technology in classrooms, are obviously way behind the times (and the expectations of students) when it comes to technology integration.

Flexible Scheduling

The disconnect between learning goals and education delivery is clearly evidenced by how the typical school day is scheduled. Breaking up the school day into forty-five-minute segments is an efficient way to deliver the curriculum and "cover" the material, but it is not effective if real learning, measured by true student engagement and deep understanding, is important. Typical school scheduling also militates against collaboration between teachers and opportunities for interdisciplinary and project-based learning. But what does scheduling have to do with school design? This book will demonstrate how the creation of *physical learning communities*— adaptable learning spaces that can be configured for the needs of various groups—can provide a wide range of scheduling choices not typically available to students and teachers in a traditional school building. A learning community looks beyond individual classrooms and classroom pairs; it defines a larger group of up to 150 students and around six to eight teachers as an operational unit where "everyone knows your name." A grouping of this size immediately breaks down the anonymity of large, impersonal, and institutional schools.

Connection to the Environment, Community, and Global Network

The school's connection to the environment, the community, and the global network is important if not critical to the delivery of a twenty-first-century education.

Connection to the environment. There is evidence that students do better in schools with more daylight, fresh air, and views of nature. Renowned environmental educator David W. Orr discusses sustainability and its importance in school design. He recommends that schools find ways "to support better alternatives that do less environmental damage, lower carbon dioxide emissions, reduce use of toxic substances, promote energy efficiency and the use of solar energy, help to build a sustainable regional economy, cut long-term costs, and provide an example to other institutions." Moreover, he adds, "the results of these studies should be woven into the curriculum as interdisciplinary courses, seminars, lectures, and research."[28]

Connection to the community. One of the problems with traditional schools is that they are so isolated from the community. However, the time for simply creating community schools is past. Community schools are traditional schools that permit a certain amount of community use after the school day. Today, schools need to serve as community learning centers where *learning* is the operative word. As I described in an earlier publication, "the community's role in this approach goes well beyond simply using school buildings after hours. Instead, community residents and institutions become active partners in education. Just as the school serves the community's interests, so also the community serves the school's purpose. School under this scheme becomes redefined as a learning center with pedagogy as a two-way street, as resources are passed back and forth between the center and the community."[29]

Connection to the global network. Traditional schools are based on a time- and space-bound, bureaucratic-hierarchical model of education. This model assumes a one-way flow of information and knowledge from the top to the bottom—and in schools this means from teacher to student. However, around the world and outside school, this model has already given way to the network model of learning. Under the network model, people connect with information, resources, and other people as needed, when needed. Here, teachers can also be learners, and learners can be teachers. A traditional school building, with its clear preference for delivery of information via lectures, is perfectly designed for the bureaucratic-hierarchical model. Thus, the structure becomes a major impediment to delivering a network model of education demanded by and prevalent in the twenty-first century.

WHAT IS THE LEARNING BUILDING?

Winston Churchill once said, "We shape our buildings; thereafter they shape us." His words reflect a universal truth that buildings start out representing the aspirations and priorities of those who design and build them, but over time, they shape the attitudes and aspirations of the people who live in them. Nowhere is this truth more evident than in the school buildings our teachers and children occupy. The overwhelming majority of school buildings represent an underlying philosophy that the Taylor industrial model of efficiency is applicable as much to students as it was for industrial workers. Under this model, learning can be defined, quantified, controlled, and mass-produced, and if that is the case, then the design of schools perfectly fits the model.

THE QUESTION OF MONEY

Surprisingly, twenty-first-century schools are almost always *less* expensive to build and operate than a traditional school. There are a number of reasons why this is so, but here are just a few:

- Twenty-first-century school facilities are more efficient because they utilize more of the built area for teaching and learning by reducing the amount of space dedicated to circulation and utilities. Almost 15 percent more space can be captured in this manner for education. Conversely, new and renovated facilities can make do with up to 15 percent less area than they might otherwise have.

- With the notion of adaptability in mind, twenty-first-century schools are built with many interior lightweight (but durable) interior walls that are less expensive to build, relocate, and remove than the heavy masonry walls that most traditional schools use.

- From my own personal experience designing schools for over twenty-five years, twenty-first-century schools are generally less likely to suffer damage due to vandalism, because students have a greater sense of ownership of the school. This reduces the cost of ongoing maintenance.

- An increase in mobile technologies means less wiring throughout the building. This advantage is especially significant in many older buildings, which still have substantial amounts of asbestos in them.

- Through joint-use agreements with community organizations and other government agencies, twenty-first-century schools can either eliminate some commons areas or create them with alternative sources of funding. This results in a substantial reduction of the capital expenditures that schools and school districts have to assume.

- The incorporation of green technologies can reduce energy consumption and reduce water use—resulting in lowered annual maintenance costs.

The second part of the Churchill quote, which suggests that those who occupy buildings begin to take on the attributes of the building, is just as easy to verify with school buildings. No one would doubt that education is delivered today in much the same way it was delivered fifty or even a hundred years ago, when industry was the engine that drove the American economy. This observation would be very troubling simply for the reason that education is stuck in the past while the rest of the world is moving on. However, the failure to keep up with the times is even more disturbing in education because this is one enterprise that, by its very nature, should be about the future. After all, the purpose of education is to equip students with the skills and competencies they need to adapt and succeed in a future world that looks very different from today's world.

Our first reaction to the defunct school-building model is to update the design of school buildings so that the design reflects today's understanding of education and current aspirations for schools. Will this solve the problem and help us create schools that better prepare students for future lives and careers? The answer is yes and no. Yes, schools designed according to today's needs would be better places for preparing students for the future than the industrial-model schools most students attend today. However, assuming that capital resources are and will always be in short supply (see the sidebar "The Question of Money"), then whatever we build or renovate today will be around for many decades to come. That means, no matter how thoughtfully we design schools today, they will continue to shape teaching and learning practice for many, many years to come. In this sense, we will simply perpetuate the problem of having future generations be shaped (in not-so-good ways) by our current model of education, which (like everything else) has a finite shelf life.

How to solve this problem? For starters, *schools need to be places that put an end to the Churchillian observation.* Churchill's comments were made at a time when buildings, once constructed, remained largely unchanged for a very long time. Thus, if the buildings were immutable, then they would obviously continue to influence many generations of people who lived and worked in them. We do not want this immutability for our schools. *We don't want today's architects telling future generations of teachers and students how to live and learn.*

To move away from the Churchillian observation, we need buildings not only to be shaped by the people who design them, but also to respond to those who live in them. In other words, we need to move away from the rigidity of the static building to the agility of the *learning building.* The thesis of this book is that a well-designed school building will look very different day to day, week to week, month to month, and year to year. The changes will be a direct result of the school occupants' shaping their learning environment to fit the needs of the learning activity the school needs to accommodate. A crude version of this idea is already at play in many schools, in the shape of the dreaded "cafetorium" or "gymnatorium"— spaces that serve different purposes. The problem is that a cafetorium, in trying to do two incompatible things, does both badly—and the same can be said for the gymnatorium.

Agility over Flexibility

The cafetorium and gymnatorium examples show that flexibility is not always a good thing. The architect's idea that some generic space can be made to work for different activities simply by moving furniture around does not work in practice. There are many qualities that make a space suitable for a particular activity. These include the extent to which it naturally lit and naturally ventilated, its outdoor connections, its size and shape, its ceiling height, how it is furnished, how well it accommodates mobile technology use, its acoustic qualities, and its use of interior finish materials and colors. An agile school building is designed so that users can have a rich variety of learning experiences but in spaces that are suitable and have the proper ambiance for the learning activity at hand, whereas a flexible school building simply focuses mostly on multiuse spaces.

The Environmentally Smart School Building

A learning building not only has to be agile, but also has to be smart. As defined here, *smart* refers to buildings that respond to both environmental conditions and user stimuli. Here are just a few examples of how a building can be smart. It would turn lights on and off as needed, maximize daylight while reducing glare, prioritize fresh air over conditioned air, reduce energy use and make consumption patterns transparent to its users, and harvest rainwater and conserve and reuse potable water. A building could also be smart in passive ways—through proper orientation to maximize daylight, the strategic placement of trees that provide shade in summer and allow in more daylight in the winter, and passive solar heating for hot water. Other passive measures include rooftop treatments like green roofs to reduce energy costs, waterless urinals, and indigenous landscaping that requires less water. Additionally, the building could expose as many of its building systems as possible so that students could understand how buildings are put together and operate.

Smart, Agile Kids

It is my firm belief that smart, agile school buildings create smart, agile kids. Research shows that the good environmental conditions smart buildings create, such as good air quality, day lighting, thermal comfort, and good acoustics, are more conducive to learning than the poor environmental conditions in which most students go to school.[30] However, being smart is not just about knowing more. It is about being a good, responsible citizen. Buildings that practice good environmental stewardship are more likely to encourage students themselves to become smarter about the use of scarce resources. Then there is the question of agility. An agile building allows teachers and students to design and implement a far greater variety of teaching and learning experiences than does a rigidly designed school building. An agile building encourages students to take greater ownership of their learning and helps foster collaboration and good learning habits that help create agile learners who will be better prepared to take on the challenges of a constantly changing world.

OVERVIEW OF THE BOOK

The ideas contained in this book are as relevant to new schools as they are to schools up for renovations. However, since the vast majority of the world's students attend school in traditional buildings, the book focuses on ways to use current spending to adapt spaces, rather than on an innovative vision for tomorrow's schools—a vision that may appear utopian and unachievable in a time of fiscal austerity.

This book is organized space by space such as classrooms, labs, and libraries, and it offers options for incremental progress while also demonstrating how all the pieces of a learning building fit together. The ideas presented draw upon my experience working with both public and private schools in the United States and around the world. The discussions are intended to address the needs of readers in many kinds of schools, with the understanding that schools have very different environments, resource levels and student needs.

Where appropriate, I have included some recurring features throughout the book. "Before and After" photo spreads show how new ideas can be put into practice, "Smart Idea" sidebars highlight particularly effective innovations, and "Do Now" sidebars feature relatively easy changes that educators can try right away in their schools.

Chapter 1, "'Reading' School Buildings," explores the visual cues that translate into messages students receive in corridors, classrooms, and common areas from elements such as acoustics, lighting, doors, furniture arrangements, wall decor, and materials available for learning. The chapter includes a sidebar on lighting and an illustrated feature on soft seating.

Chapter 2 talks about the importance of school entries and how these can be designed to be welcoming. A checklist for assessing your school's entries is included as well as a "Smart Idea" feature on signature elements.

FIGURE I.5 *Before:* Teacher-centered classroom at P. K. Yonge Developmental Research School at the University of Florida in Gainesville.

FIGURE I.6 *After:* Student-centered learning commons at the new P. K. Yonge School completed in the fall of 2012.

FIGURE I.7 *Before:* Hallway at the International School of Brussels before a summer renovation as a temporary high school.

FIGURE I.8 *After:* The design of the same area into a learning community with this commons space now allows multiple forms of learning not previously possible.

Chapter 3, "Capturing More Space for Learning," discusses how classrooms and hallways can be redesigned to create learning communities and how the substantial amount of space wasted by hallways can be captured for teaching and learning use. The chapter lists twenty essential modalities of learning that school buildings need to support and a "Smart Idea" section on partitions.

Chapter 4 discusses labs, specialty studios, and do-it-yourself spaces and introduces some not-so-familiar terms to the school community. Integrated learning areas like the Da Vinci studio, the espresso studio, and the Jamie Oliver studio are described. The chapter also includes a "Smart Idea" sidebar on the kiva, another innovative idea for school spaces.

Chapter 5, "Making Room for Collaboration," discusses how school design can support teachers. It contains a "Smart Idea" feature on how to create a low-cost focal space for teachers.

Chapter 6 talks about the changing face of the school library and how it can become an effective place for putting people and ideas together in today's technological world. One "Smart Idea" sidebar describes changes that schools can make immediately to their outdated libraries to bring them more in line with today's needs.

Chapter 7, "Beyond the Classroom Window," focuses on outdoor learning. It looks at elements such as connecting with nature, play, learning terraces, and creating green areas in urban settings.

Chapter 8 describes how institutional cafeterias can be converted to more community-centered cafés and provides a case study and an illustrated feature on kitchen gardens.

The conclusion of the book, "Putting Theory into Practice," provides ideas for how schools can begin transforming their facilities. Specific case studies offered here show how the principles and strategies discussed throughout this book can be implemented.

In appendixes A and B, at the end of the book, I have provided two school evaluation checklists, one for elementary school facilities and one for secondary school facilities. These represent a hybrid tool based on Lorraine Maxwell's "Classroom Assessment Scale" and Fielding Nair International's "Educational Facilities Effectiveness Instrument."[31]

ON A PERSONAL NOTE . . .

I feel uniquely qualified to write this book because I have, literally, "served on both sides of the aisle" as an architect responsible for creating both traditional and innovative, twenty-first-century schools. For ten years, from 1989 to 1999, I served as the director of operations for New York City's school construction program. In this role, I participated in the design and construction of nearly $10 billion worth of projects that included the creation of over one hundred new schools and the completion of more than six hundred renovation projects. Having had a direct and personal involvement in these projects, I can say with complete conviction that none of the projects built or renovated during my tenure in New York City would fit the definition of a twenty-first-century school.

The massive infusion of funds succeeded in bringing the city's schools into a state of good repair and met the most basic requirement of a school facility, which is to keep students safe, warm, and dry. Beyond that, however, nothing fundamentally changed with the way in which education was being delivered in the city. School buildings did not facilitate new ways to teach and learn, and neither did they serve as a catalyst for true education reform. The new and renovated buildings we created simply extended what we now know is a defunct cells-and-bells educational model. Sadly, built as they were to last fifty years or more, New York City's stock of new and renovated school buildings will adversely impact the city's ability to deliver a true twenty-first-century education for many decades to come.

After I left government service, I took a one-year sabbatical from architecture to work for a national technology company coordinating the implementation of one-on-one computing programs (one computer for every student) for schools across the United States. It was during this period that I met many innovative educators who were using the influx of technology into schools as a catalyst to move to a more student-centered model of teaching and learning. Despite these educators' notable successes, it was apparent to me that their efforts were being seriously thwarted by the design of their factory-model school buildings.

When I returned to the field of educational architecture in 2001, I did so as an independent practitioner intent on bringing what I had learned from my educator colleagues to the architectural profession. My goal was to close the wide chasm that existed between educational research and school architecture so that buildings could be designed from the ground up or renovated to facilitate rather than hinder good educational practice.

In the early years of my return to architecture, I found many eager clients who had themselves been frustrated by the limits on good teaching and learning imposed by traditional school buildings. In 2003, I joined forces with my business partner Randall Fielding, and, together, over the past ten years, we have taken our ideas to schools throughout the United States and to many other countries around the world. By 2014, our practice had expanded to cover forty-three countries on six continents. What I have learned in my second career focused exclusively on the development of innovative schools designed to meet the needs of the twenty-first century is that good school design is something everyone needs but also something few people know how to ask for. I also learned that for all the impact our practice as innovative architects has had, it represents barely a ripple in the sea of traditional schools that continue to be built to this day. From my own personal experience, I would estimate that over 99 percent of school buildings being constructed or reno-vated today across the globe would qualify as traditional, twentieth-century facili-ties. Thus, the need to get the word out to a wider audience that there is a better way to design schools has never been greater.

This book is written so that all school stakeholders, and educators in particular, can understand the difference between a traditional school building and a facility designed to meet the needs of today's and tomorrow's learners. I will also show that it takes no more effort, money, or time to create a twenty-first-century school than is currently expended to perpetuate the obsolete factory-model school.

The overall theme of this book is how the design of learning places can reflect and embrace the rapid changes in twenty-first-century education—which is what the learning building is all about.

CHAPTER ONE

"Reading" School Buildings

A Visual Literacy Primer

FOR THE PURPOSES of this book, *visual literacy* is defined as a deep understanding of what one sees. A case can be made that most people "see" school buildings but do not really understand them. Before we can do anything to improve schools, we first need to understand how profoundly the buildings in which they are housed affect their occupants.

The schoolhouse is possibly the most iconic element of American architecture, and yet, perhaps for that very same reason, it is also the most invisible. This chapter will take the cloak of invisibility off the school building, allowing everyone to see it for what it actually is. In the process, readers will learn to decode the subtle and not-so-subtle messages that a school building sends to its occupants. These messages are so powerful that they have a profound impact on everyone who occupies the building and everything that happens within its four walls.

The good news is that the uniformity of school designs affords opportunities for generalizable solutions to the problems these designs present. However, just as it is hard to separate language and grammar if you only speak one language, it's hard for educators to realize that the physical "grammar" of schooling could be quite different from the one they know. For that to happen, they literally to have to look at familiar school buildings with fresh eyes.

A VISUAL LITERACY TOUR OF YOUR NEIGHBORHOOD SCHOOL

Come take an abbreviated tour of your neighborhood school with me. As you enter the building, does it feel welcoming? Is the entry freshly painted with warm colors and perhaps a signature decorative feature that celebrates the school's culture or history? Did someone greet you as soon as you walked through the door? Is there a place for visitors to sit comfortably, with perhaps coffee, magazines, or fresh flowers and a place to hang a coat? What kinds of student work are on display—is there space for presentation of complex projects? All these elements bespeak pride in the school as it "introduces" itself to the visitor.

The journey you take to a child's classroom is significant because it is one he or she takes every day. On this journey, there are messages being sent to your child, many far more powerful and visceral than anything a teacher might say. The design of this space will directly influence either good behavior or bad behavior simply by virtue of its visual cues. These are the ones you are looking for. Are displays at an adult height or at a height where children can delight in them? Is the corridor dark or well lit—or even better, is it day-lit? Is there a clear view into the classrooms, or are they completely locked away from view?

As you enter a typical classroom, look at how the room is arranged. Is there a variety of spaces where children can work in groups of various sizes or alone? Can the space be easily reconfigured to adapt to different needs (lecture, group work, independent study)? Is the whiteboard low enough so that students can write on it? (This tells students immediately if the room is for them or for the adult.) Are children able to use wireless technology, or are they limited to one or two computers at the back of the room? Is there soft seating in the classroom and space for children to sit and work comfortably on the floor?

Then look at how the room connects to other learning spaces (or doesn't). Does the room connect to an outdoor learning terrace? Does it connect to the classroom next door, and if so, are the two teachers working together? Does the classroom open onto the corridor through operable glass doors so that students can be visually supervised as they work in the hallway?

Educators and parents need to ask questions like these if they want to understand whether the learning environment in which children spend most of their waking day meets the four design principles of being welcoming, being versatile, supporting varied learning activities, and sending positive behavioral messages. These qualities are conducive to learning and, just as important, to children's overall health and well-being.

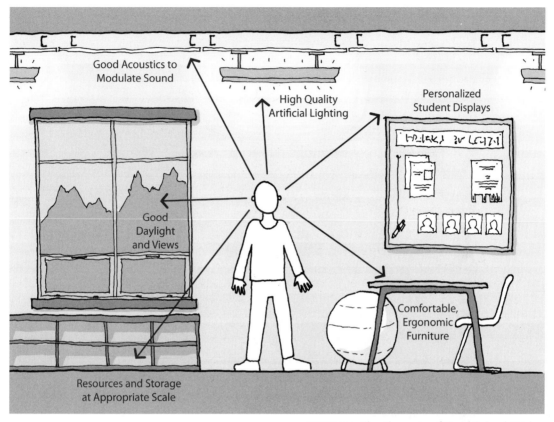

Good Acoustics to Modulate Sound

High Quality Artificial Lighting

Personalized Student Displays

Good Daylight and Views

Comfortable, Ergonomic Furniture

Resources and Storage at Appropriate Scale

FIGURE 1.1 The Elements of Good School Design

DESIGN ELEMENTS THAT DEFINE EDUCATIONAL EFFECTIVENESS

Now let's delve deeper into how various elements of a school's design influence the school's educational effectiveness. The design elements that need to be considered and applied thoughtfully both in the design of new schools and in the renovation of existing schools can be grouped into five categories:[1]

- Spatial organization
- The learning environment
- Personalization
- Technology
- Interior design

FIGURE 1.2 This learning studio at Lake Country School in Minneapolis is different from a typical classroom. The furnishings are varied to allow for a variety of learning modes. The room has ample daylight and storage, and the blackboard has been lowered, so that it can be used by both teachers and students.

The following sections examine the design elements that make up each of these five categories, beginning with key visual cues to identify whether the element is properly deployed in school. Further details are then provided for those who want to have a more complete understanding of any particular design element.

SPATIAL ORGANIZATION

Spatial organization includes elements dealing with how the physical space in a school is organized. For schools to work well, it is important not only that they have adequate space but also that the space is organized properly to benefit learning.

Spatial organization includes scale, variety and flexibility of space, and informal learning areas.

Scale

For visual cues relating to scale, look for doors that children can open, toilets that they can use without adult help, windows with sills that are low enough for them to look out of, and furniture that is appropriately sized and lightweight enough for them to move on their own.[2]

Scale refers to different things for different age groups. For very young children, scale refers to the design of their learning environment at a scale that is accessible to them and their needs. Scale also pertains to the balance of elements in the school as a whole. For older buildings with multiple renovations, look to see if entrances feel small and cramped even in schools with several thousand students. On the other hand, if you are in a newer school, check to see if the building has large, architecturally impressive atriums that tend to get very little actual use.

The scale of traditional schools buildings fails at many levels. The most significant problem is the classroom whose scale is almost always inappropriate for the number of students who occupy it. To get a sense of how little space each student has in a 750-square-foot classroom with twenty-five students, just walk into a classroom and look at how it is organized. In particular, note all the furniture that is crammed into the room and how much space is taken up by the teacher's desk. The actual remaining space that each student can claim as his or her own is less than what prisoners in a high-security prison cell are allocated.

The scale of other areas of the school paints an equally depressing picture. Centralized bathrooms are too large and corridors are too narrow and long—both magnets for bullying and other antisocial behavior. Cafeterias are impersonal cattle sheds—large and noisy with few redeeming qualities except that they can feed large numbers of students in a short time. Social spaces where students can gather comfortably in small numbers are either absent altogether or too few and too small to meet the needs of the school population. These are the problems that we can begin to address once our visual literacy is honed to the point where the sorry state of our school buildings will no longer be invisible.

Variety and Flexibility

To understand more about variety and flexibility, walk around the school to assess if spaces are set up to permit a multiplicity of learning activities. Are students and

FIGURE 1.3   It is important to provide a variety of seating options. This image from the International School of Brussels shows bench seating, bar stool seating, regular ergonomic chairs, and soft seating.

teachers able to easily change the look and feel of a space? Is there a rich variety of spaces located at the heart of academic areas, or are these "zoned" in different parts of the school, making them harder to access when needed and as needed?

The provision of a multitude of possibilities within one space is essential to promote real flexibility. This flexibility is particularly important, given the need to personalize learning settings and respond to the increasing mobility of students, as advancements in technology allow for learning to occur "anywhere, anytime."[3] A variety of materials, tools, and furnishings allows students and teachers to change the way a space looks and how it is used. Variety facilitates a sense of competency in young children and is also shown to be good for older students, as both younger and older students tend to prefer furnishings whose use they have control over.[4]

A review by the University of Newcastle and the Design Council (UK) concludes that the most successful school designs generally have the elements of flexibility and adaptability, allowing for changes in curriculum, future technology, future cohorts of learners, and teaching staff.[5]

Traditional school buildings are very simple and very predictable. One reason for this is that they lack a variety of spaces. If you count the different kinds of spaces consciously set aside for learning in any school, you will find that a majority of the so-called learning is supposed to occur in evenly sized classrooms containing a set number of students each. Then there are the labs, which are slightly larger—but only to accommodate the equipment they contain. A few small group rooms are sometimes set aside to deal with children who need special assistance. Beyond that, there are many specialty rooms, each designed for a particular purpose. These include the cafeteria, the gymnasium, the auditorium, music rooms, art rooms, and the like. Compare this to a children's museum, which is defined by variety—variety of spaces, variety of displays, variety of experiences, and variety of opportunities for natural inter-age learning.[6] Sadly, schools are at the opposite end of the spectrum when it comes to a design that naturally promotes learning.

Informal Learning Areas: The "Third Place"

Psychologists describe the *third place* as a setting outside home and work where socializing, eating and drinking, reading, studying, and relaxing in the company of others happens.[7] The third place is where informal learning occurs. Therefore it is important that all learning environments allow for social and informal interaction to take place.

Walk around the school, and look for students engaged in informal learning. This sort of learning happens when students interact socially with each other, help one another out with homework assignments, or work independently. It may happen during breaks between classes, during recess and lunch, and sometimes even during regular class periods. You may see students working in ones and twos in hallways, in stairwells, under a tree, on the grass, and wherever they can find a place to sit—all outside the formal environment of the classroom.

Then ask yourself, how much of the informal learning that occurs in a school takes place in spaces that the architect consciously designed for such activities? If this question were to be applied to a traditional school building, the answer would be, "Very little." Some of the more recently designed school buildings do pay closer attention to the need for informal learning spaces outside classrooms and are more successful in this regard.

FIGURE 1.4 This outdoor deck illustrates the function of the "third place" as an informal space for students to gather and work together casually.

THE LEARNING ENVIRONMENT

Three key environmental factors have a direct impact on learning: thermal comfort and air quality, lighting, and acoustics. For the layperson, visual cues relating to thermal comfort and air quality will be less apparent, although thermal comfort is something most building occupants directly experience as being either good or bad. Fixes in this area mostly relate to the engineering of the building, which is outside the scope of this book. However, from the perspective of improved air quality, it is a safe generalization that operable windows that bring in fresh air are almost always preferable to sealed windows. As a visual literacy cue, look for closed windows on days when the weather outside is good—windows are often closed in these conditions—and suggest to teachers that they keep windows open so kids can breathe fresh air. In this chapter, I discuss two design elements related to the learning environment: lighting and acoustics.

Lighting

From a visual literacy standpoint, the most important thing to observe with regard to lighting is the extent to which every key learning area has a substantial amount of daylight. As a general rule, the more daylight any particular space gets, the better it will be for learning. Second, areas that are artificially lit should be bright enough for the activities that happen within them. Third, areas that have multiple uses—particularly after-hours use, should be well lit for both daytime and evening use.

From a learning standpoint, few aspects of a school design are as important as lighting and acoustics, yet these areas are mostly overlooked by educators. The most valuable kind of light that a student can have in schools is daylight, and every effort has to be made to increase daylight in student-occupied areas.

In some situations, daylight needs to be managed. These include times when there is need for less light for electronic presentations and when direct sunlight

SHEDDING LIGHT ON LIGHTING

Most artificial light found in schools comes from fluorescent light fixtures that are embedded in ceilings. The best light for learning is one that closely approximates sunlight, referenced by the selected lamp's color rendition index (CRI). For spaces that are used both in the evening and during the day, a good lighting design will include a variety of light fixtures to accommodate different levels of brightness and ambiances. In these areas, the change in lighting can change the mood and ambiance of a space when it is goes from an academic setting to a community event setting, for example. Some people exposed to fluorescent lights experience drowsiness, headaches, migraines, and difficulty in concentration. The best remedy for these difficulties is to ensure that areas lit by fluorescent lights are also day-lit.* In the future, this problem is likely to go away with the introduction of extremely energy-efficient LED lighting. In the meantime, replacing fixtures with better-quality lamps and ballasts will often solve some of the health problems just noted.†

*Seattle Community Network (SCN), "Fluorescent Lighting and Other Optical Issues: Adaptations," SCN web page, last modified March 6, 2013, www.scn.org/autistics/fluorescents.html.
†Power Sleuth, "Recommended Light Levels," Student Handout 9.1 (Augusta, ME: PowerSleuth, 2009), www.powersleuth.org/docs/EnergyLightsMaine-Handout9_1.pdf.

creates glare in the learning environment. The proper and limited use of blinds will solve this problem—but without being educated about the benefits of daylight, teachers will often close blinds for most of the school day and just use artificial light instead.

Acoustics

It is easy to visually assess whether a space will be acoustically comfortable. The most important thing to look for, particularly in schools, which are full of sound-reflecting surfaces, is the evidence of sound-absorption surfaces and materials. That means soft or permeable surfaces that will absorb rather than reflect sound: for example, acoustic ceilings, cork and similar materials on wall surfaces, and soft seating.

Classroom Acoustics. The acoustical quality of learning environments like classrooms is important because it determines how well a child is able to hear and understand what an adult is saying.[8] Classrooms tend to have mostly reflective surfaces and very few sound-absorbing surfaces. This environment makes classrooms noisy, forces teachers to speak very loudly in order to be heard, and creates a very bad environment for any kind of small-group work because conversations from one table are heard at adjoining tables. A quick fix to these problems involves the introduction of more sound-absorbing materials into the room. Usually this is accomplished by bringing in soft seating and perhaps lining walls with Tectum acoustical panels or panels wrapped in sound-absorbing fabric. Most classrooms in the United States have acoustical ceilings, but wherever these are missing, some treatment of the ceiling may also be necessary. The introduction of carpet into the classroom has also been shown to reduce the impact of the sounds of foot traffic, moving chairs, and even fidgeting.[9] However, where there are concerns with maintenance, carpet tiles that can be easily installed and replaced are a viable option.

Using alternative teaching methods and furniture arrangements that reduce the distance between students and teachers has been shown to significantly improve classroom acoustics.[10] While trees are definitely not a short-term fix, the presence of trees outside classroom windows is good not only because trees connect students with nature but because they also shield the school from outside noises like traffic.

Learning Communities and Acoustics. Where classrooms and hallways are combined to create learning communities (more on this subject in chapter 4), acoustics takes on far greater importance. Not only could acoustics become a make-or-break issue for the very notion of creating learning communities, in practice, learning communities present a whole different set of operational challenges that have direct implications for acoustical design. In such cases, a very conscious effort has to be made to design the acoustics of the space. The services of an acoustician are recommended to review the design, do "reverb" calculations (to ensure that sound quality is acceptable), and suggest changes where appropriate.

Acoustics in Other Parts of the School. As a general rule, schools tend to have more reflective surfaces (since these surfaces are easier to clean) than sound-absorbing surfaces. This is particularly true in spaces like cafeterias and gymnasiums. Again, making these spaces more livable means introducing more sound-absorbing materials. Cafeterias may need a different kind of flooring (like cork or wood) that has better sound absorption than vinyl flooring and the introduction of ceiling-hung acoustic panels or "clouds" that can also have decorative value. Walls can be treated with acoustic materials, and the room can be furnished with some easy-to-clean cafeteria furniture with better sound-absorbing qualities than traditional hard-plastic and metal furniture.

PERSONALIZATION

Students spend most of their waking day in schools, yet there is very little in school that they can call their own and few places where they can be on their own. Just as adults in offices need their own work space and privacy, so also do children need places in school that they can personalize and where they can be alone. The elements of personalization include privacy, a home base, and individual storage.

Interesting thought

Privacy

All human beings (including young children) have a need for privacy—to get away from the crowd and be alone. Schools, however, are often the worst places for privacy because they assume that the security of children is incompatible with privacy.

It is not difficult to visually observe whether a school provides needed privacy for students. Look for places where students can be alone with their thoughts. Preferably, these areas should be consciously designed for independent study, quiet reading, using a mobile computer, or just relaxing. Keep in mind the total number of students in the school, and ask yourself if areas for privacy are adequate to serve the full student population.

From a design standpoint, there are three specific types of places in which students can have the privacy they need to be good learners and good citizens.

Places to Be Alone. Design can consciously create nooks where students can retreat to be alone to work, relax, eat, listen to music, or read. These places do not have to be visibly private as long as students who occupy such areas feel comfortable that they are alone and undisturbed. Such areas are sometimes found in school libraries, but most schools are sadly lacking in other areas where students can be alone. Another obvious area where students need privacy is the bathroom. Privacy here also refers to a student's comfort that he or she will not be bullied. Therefore, bathrooms should be smaller in scale (three to five urinals and stalls, maximum) and located where adults can easily supervise students going in and out of them.

Places to Converse in Private with a Friend. Social discourse is an important part of the informal learning process.[11] Like the individual nooks described above, places can be consciously designed for two students to talk or work with each other without being disturbed by others. These areas can also be used for a teacher to work one-on-one with a student who needs extra help or tutoring.

Places to Nourish the Mind and Spirit. These "restorative areas" are very important for both student and teachers to offset the effects of mental fatigue through stress reduction, relaxation, reflection, and rest.[12] A restorative space allows for reflection and facilitates creativity.[13] Stephen Kaplan, codeveloper of the attention restoration theory, outlines key characteristics of restorative spaces as follows:

> *Sense of being away:* The space must be a place other than the source of the fatigue.
> *Extent:* The place is different, feels like another world, with stimuli different from the usual.
> *Fascination:* The space must provide enough to see so that the mind is taken away from thoughts connected to the source of mental fatigue. "Soft fascinations" are most directly related to nature and are objects that gain attention with little effort. An example is someone's watching leaves rustle in the wind.
> *Compatibility:* The place must be a good fit to a person's inclinations, meaning that he or she would instinctively know how to act without struggle and without a need to learn how to behave.[14]

Ideally, these spaces should be connected with nature—if only a window seat facing the trees or sky.[15] Issues of security can be addressed by having the area passively supervised by adults and enclosed within glass walls.

Restorative Spaces [handwritten margin note]

A Home Base

Ideally all students should have both a home base and a place to store their belongings. Elementary school students have the luxury of a dedicated desk that they can call their own. As students move through middle and high school, they often become nomads and have no dedicated place to work at or store their belongings except for a student locker. In a traditional secondary school, almost all of the space is unowned—a situation that can increase the incidence of vandalism.

Schools need to do a better job of providing students with a home base. Those that follow the advisory model sometimes give every student his or her own personal workstation, which the student occupies for much of the school day, just as people in the workplace do. The advisory or home-base model typically refers to

FIGURE 1.5 These personalized student cubbies at Shorecrest Prep School in Saint Petersburg, Florida, are sized so that students can move them easily. The cubbies are also located below the windowsills so as not to block daylight and views to the deck and playground outside.

an organizational grouping of ten to fifteen students and one advisor or teacher who meet regularly and typically work together on projects. For example, there could be several clusters of individual student workstations adjacent to commons and other activity areas.[16] Most schools cannot afford to provide individual work-stations but can come up with creative solutions so that each student has a sense of ownership for the school and doesn't feel as if he or she is part of an anonymous institution.

TECHNOLOGY

Given the history of schools as places to mass-produce learning, technology offers an opportunity to provide each student with opportunities for a more personal learning experience. Elements relating to technology include opportunities and constraints of the building design and learning beyond the classroom.

Very little has been written about the influence of school design on the way technology is deployed or used in schools. The following five questions can help you investigate whether the design of a building facilitates or hinders the use of technology as a transformative learning tool.

Does the building design dictate how technology is deployed? Do you have to go into classrooms to see technology being used, because there are no collaborative areas where this might happen? Are there more desktops in the school than laptops? Are whiteboards used mostly as a lecturing aid by teachers? Are there computer labs where students go to learn how to use technology? Is student use of technology mostly at the discretion of teachers?

How is technology being used, and how often is it being used? Is technology being used throughout the school day in all subject areas? Is it being used for interdisci-plinary projects? Are students simply consuming digital content, or are they also creating it? Is there evidence of high-end uses of technology like programming and the production of industry-standard creative outputs like graphic-arts projects, publications, and computer apps?[17] To what extent are these extended uses of tech-nology precluded by the lack of adequate or appropriate spaces in the school?

Is there a range of technologies in evidence? Do students have access to Internet-connected desktops for quick research? Are there dedicated areas where such easy-access desktops can be located? Do they have ready access to laptops? Are there secure places where laptop carts can be plugged in for charging? Is there evidence that students are using video and digital cameras as an integral part of their school-work? Is there secure storage for such devices close to academic areas, or do students have to travel to some central location like a library? Are the computers in school of recent vintage, and do students know and use the latest software? Are mobile devices like student-owned smartphones and tablets used for schoolwork?[18]

Is technology enabling learning beyond classrooms? Is there wireless access throughout the school? Is there an adequate number of wireless access points to cover the whole school, or are there blackout zones with no coverage? Does the design of spaces enable students to use computers and other technologies in school when they need it and where they need it, in the same way that they might use it outside school?[19]

How can better outcomes be achieved with a twenty-first-century school design? This is an opportunity to juxtapose technology use and school building design. You should ask how the design of the school either limits or facilitates the use of technology. Beyond simply looking at technology as a tool to do traditional education better, you need to see technology (just like the buildings themselves) as a key change agent to transform education from a teacher-centered model to a student-centered model.

INTERIOR DESIGN

Interior design includes all the things that most adults care deeply about in all aspects of their daily lives. Whether it is the homes in which they live, the places where they work, the restaurants where they eat and socialize, the stores where they shop and the hotels where they stay, design represents all the things that make these places livable and usable. Of course, beyond basic functionality, interior design also make the experiences in all these places more pleasant and enjoyable. A little known observation about good interior design is that it can improve people's health and well-being and make them more productive.[20] Unfortunately, schools rarely benefit from good design, possibly because of the mistaken impression that good design is a luxury for students. In fact, this assumption is far from the case. A comfortable chair to sit in and a pleasant environment to learn are not luxuries in school any more than they would be in the workplace. We will look at several elements of interior design: furnishings, colors, materials, textures, clutter, ethos, and aesthetics.

Furnishings

Walk around a typical school, and look closely at the furniture that is being used throughout the building. A well-designed school will use furniture that is ergonomic, comfortable, and carefully selected to match the learning activities that happen in any given space. Furniture for students should match the same high standards you would have for furnishing your own home or office.

Furnishings are one of the most important elements of good school design and are absolutely critical for creating a twenty-first-century learning environment. Yet, they are also one of the most overlooked. It is not hard to find schools that cost $100 million or more to build but were outfitted with $30 to $50 chairs for students. When it comes to the physical aspects of schooling, there is perhaps nothing more important than the student chair. Students sit in chairs—usually cheap, hard plastic chairs—for four to six hours each day. Multiply that by the number of school days times the number of years a student spends in school to understand how important this one piece of furniture is. Rarely are the chairs that students sit on ergonomically designed. Ergonomic chairs or chairs that allow for movement can improve concentration. In fact, there is a whole field of study, called *cognitive ergonomics*, concerned with mental processes, such as perception, memory, and reasoning and how these are affected by our physical environment.[21]

Of course, one goal of twenty-first-century schooling is to have students spend less time in a chair than they do now. Hellerup School in Finland came up with a good solution to this problem. The total number of chairs in the school equals 50 percent of the total number of students. That means students cannot, on average, spend more than 50 percent of their school day sitting in a chair. So what do students do when they are not sitting in a chair? Learning areas include stools, exercise balls, and soft seating like armchairs or couches and beanbags, or even just space for students to work while standing or while sitting on the floor.

A good furnishings plan must be prepared in coordination with the floor plan of the school itself. If we start with the assumption that a variety of learning spaces are good because they encourage a variety of learning activities, then it follows that a school will have much more variety in the furnishings it specifies than is currently the norm (see the sidebar "Smart Idea: A Variety of Furnishings").

It is tempting to dismiss the need for appropriate furniture as excessive and unnecessary or to assume that it is simply unaffordable. One option is to get quality used furniture from the business sector—many companies are happy to donate

SMART IDEA: A VARIETY OF FURNISHINGS

Here is a sample list of furniture you might expect to see in a twenty-first-century school:

- Ergonomic chairs
- Rocking chairs
- Ball chairs
- Chairs on wheels
- Beanbags
- Student desks that can be arranged in groups
- Adjustable-height tables
- Worktables
- Café tables
- Stools—different styles
- Armchairs
- Couches
- Soft sectionals—with multiple arrangement options
- Benches
- Bistro tables and chairs for outdoors

FIGURES 1.6 & 1.7 Ergonomic seating may include unconventional options such as the ball chair and the Hokki stool. Both allow for movement while remaining stable, and both are ergonomically designed. Ergonomic seating is not only good for student health and well-being but also helpful for concentration and academic performance.

FIGURE 1.8 A variety of furnishings used in this commons area at the P. K. Yonge Developmental Research School at the University of Florida in Gainesville makes the space more functional, comfortable, and aesthetically pleasing.

their older furniture to schools. The sad fact is that used business furniture is often better than brand-new school furniture.

Furniture should be easy to use, easy to move, and easy to personalize for the changing activities, users, and needs. When learners are able to manage their environment, they shape it to support the manner in which they work best.[22]

Colors

Children will almost always prefer colorful environments over plain ones. However, most schools pay little attention to color. Environments for older students have very little color, and young children's environments are decorated with primary and other saturated colors. Neither option is good. For color to be effective, it needs to be carefully selected.

Color has an impact on learning. Many studies have found that color influences student behavior, attitudes, productivity, academic achievement, and attention span and even affects teachers' sense of time.[23] Negative effects of monotone environments have been reported and include anxiety, depression, irritability, and an inability to concentrate. For walls, lighter palettes should be favored over darker ones to make rooms brighter and reflect more daylight, although it is OK to have some accent colors to liven up the environment. Front wall, or "teaching wall" treatments of a medium hue adjacent to more neutral-colored walls are a way to reduce eye strain and increase focus and brain activity.[24]

For very young children, primary colors can be overstimulating and are not recommended. Bright colors can be reserved for stairways and corridors to provide variety and stimulation and to aid in way-finding.[25] Using color and graphics for way-finding is particularly important for younger children, as they are able to attach significance and meaning to specific colors and symbols.[26] The use of color and graphics for way-finding encourages place identity and a sense of security and allows children to confidently navigate their environment.

The idea is to use color in ways that complement a space's intended purposes and that will create mentally and emotionally uplifting environments.[27]

Materials and Textures

Given the amount of time that students spend in classrooms, it is important that they be interesting places where a variety of activities can be supported. Toward this goal, the school should have some variety in the classroom surfaces like walls and floors and even ceilings. Tack boards should be available to display student work; whiteboards and specially painted walls can serve as writing surfaces; and substantial sections can be made of glass to let in daylight, create views to nature, and provide transparency to interior and outside areas.

Floor surfaces should vary to accommodate different activities. Carpets and area rugs are good for floor seating, linoleum can be used in wet and messy areas, and wood floors are good for active areas.

Clutter

Students learn best in uncluttered environments. With the finest of intentions, however, teachers often go overboard in decorating their classrooms to the point where there is no free wall space. Even the glass windows are often covered with displays preventing valuable daylight from entering the room. In classrooms for younger children, mobiles are hung from ceilings, and there is an abundance of teaching and learning materials everywhere.

According to Lorraine Maxwell, "tidiness" is important for students not just because it helps create spaces that are "restorative," but also because a well-organized space allows students to have more control over their environment and helps build autonomy.[28]

Ethos and Aesthetics

If you were blindfolded and dropped into a typical school anywhere in the country, it would be nearly impossible to guess where you were after the blindfold was removed. The uniformity of school designs across North America is nothing short of scary.

Every community has a history, a story to tell, people and times to be proud about. Every community also defines itself by something in its present that gives the community its unique identity. From the time a person sets foot within a neighborhood school to the visit to the last classroom in the building, a school should live and breathe the essence of the community in which it resides. This self-identity can be accomplished in many ways: the use of the name of the school; the display of signature elements such as artwork and sculpture on the school grounds, including the entry; the choice of building materials and the craftsmanship of the school's various elements; names assigned to different blocks or rooms; and the use of color—all these features can give the building a sense of place. Features like these speak to the heart and soul of the community itself.

To Clutter or Not to Clutter

FIGURE 1.9 This early-childhood classroom shows how teachers will often go overboard with displays and mobiles and even tape up windows with student work. Not only does this kind of clutter reduce the effectiveness of the space, but it also lacks the restorative qualities needed in a good learning environment.

FIGURE 1.10 See how this space, by being organized and uncluttered, is more functional and more restorative.

CHAPTER TWO

A Welcoming Message

Entries and Common Areas

NOWHERE IS THE DICTUM "first impression counts" more true than when it comes to the entry of a typical school. The experience of entering a building powerfully influences the way a person feels inside it.

As we enter any building—and schools are no exception to this rule—we shed our public "street" persona just as we remove our outerwear and adapt our behavior to the indoors, where there is an expectation that the people we encounter have something in common with us. This transition can be stressful to a visitor for a number of reasons. The more severe and institutional the entry, the more it demands that visitors adopt behaviors such as deference to rules and the assumption of a more formal attitude. Visitors may wonder whether they will find their destination easily and feel the anxiety of being lost. Whether a visitor feels welcome or intimidated is entirely a function of design.

For students, the entry experience is amplified even further. How and where a student enters the school sets the tone for his or her whole day. The design principles of being welcoming and sending positive messages are especially relevant here. Through thoughtful design, we can introduce visual and spatial cues that provide a sense of place and belonging for all who arrive and that set a pleasurable tone for their visit. Arriving at school should be educational, engaging students, staff, and visitors in a positive, social way.

ENTERING SCHOOL IS THE START OF A JOURNEY

Let's look at entering a school as a journey, which begins at the arrival onto school property by foot, bus, or car. School bus areas should be set away from the school entrance to afford fresh air, sunlight, and other natural elements to the students as they walk to the entrance.[1] Clear signage that directs visitors to the entrance from parking areas is especially necessary if the visitors must proceed to an entrance not directly in view. Landscaping and walkways of expanding widths can also assist people to naturally flow to the entry and ease the strain of way-finding. Where space permits, rain gardens and native vegetation offer inexpensive ways to create a welcoming, natural atmosphere for visitors and students alike and can also partly

SMART IDEA: SIGNATURE ELEMENTS

One of the raps on school design is how generic and institutional it tends to be. Of course, school districts cannot afford to custom-design every school to be unique to its neighborhood and reflect the ethos of its community. However, it is still important to introduce one or more signature elements into each school to give the school its own identity. Students place great importance on these signature elements since these features make the school special and different. Often, these elements become a source of pride and ownership—both key components to build a positive school climate. Signature elements should be memorable and iconic and, ideally, relate to some aspect of the school or its community's character, history, or ethos.

FIGURE 2.1 This large signature mural featuring students at the American School of Bombay is prominently located in the school's central commons area, which is accessed from a ceremonial stair.

screen parking areas from the views within the school learning spaces. Visitors and students are thus led via the most pleasant route possible to the main entry.

Because school entrances are often approached from more than one direction, it is particularly important that they be visible from an extreme side view as well as from the front. An overhang or gabled roof that projects well over the entry doors is one excellent solution to achieve this goal. It provides weather protection and a place for students to congregate or wait for transportation safely.

When a wide range of grade levels shares a building, separating the entrances by age is important so that younger children are not hurt or intimidated by the rush of older students attempting to get into or out of the building. For very young children,

FIGURE 2.2 The koi pond at Sinarmas World Academy in Indonesia is a dramatic and pleasing signature element with an environmentally friendly message. It is located at the school's academic entry.

FIGURE 2.3 The main entry of this middle school on the Scotch Oakburn College campus in Tasmania, Australia, features a signature amphitheater that was constructed with locally quarried stone.

FIGURE 2.4 The tree house at the Anne Frank Inspire Academy in San Antonio, Texas, rests on a 200-year old tree. The structure is the first of its kind in the United States and represents a distinctive signature element of a campus that celebrates outdoor learning.

entries should be located so that parents can either walk them to the door easily or safely hand them off to teachers and staff, who can then walk them to the student entry.

Outdoor areas that are immediately adjacent to the main entrance doors provide an opportunity to exhibit school pride and student accomplishment through the display of artwork, sculpture, fountains, and welcoming signage. Signature elements that embrace the community's local ethos invite residents to participate as volunteers in school or support special school events (see the sidebar "Smart Idea:

FIGURE 2.5   Meadowdale Middle School is set in a forest of native evergreens in Lynnwood, Washington, and incorporates lots of wood in the façade as a signature element. This two-storied entry and overhang creates a casual outdoor gathering space in the wet Pacific Northwest climate.

Signature Elements"). A digital display behind the windows might intersperse a calendar of happenings with student video projects or news. One of my projects, in Regina, Saskatchewan, creates educational campuses that also serve the community, particularly the First Nations people. For this reason, the art, colors, and other materials used in the entrances invite the neighborhood in, particularly the tribal elders. This kind of customization makes school entries read like places where the community feels welcome.

In too many schools, the immediate space in front of the main school entrance is utilitarian, designed to allow people to pour into the building as quickly as possible, with little social interaction. Not only is such an approach unwelcoming, it also creates an abrupt change from the outside to the inside—a change that can be stressful for those who make this transition on a regular basis. A better solution would be to make the transition gradually, with a shift in grade, a split to two pathways, or a change in surface materials before the entry path arrives at the entrance area. Adjacent to the entrance, a social area with casual resting places like steps deep enough for seating and benches can offer welcome places to eat lunch or wait for a friend out of the sun. This informal, unrushed environment allows students, parents, and other visitors to feel comfortable pausing to have a conversation, finish a cup of coffee, or wait for colleagues on the steps before they actually enter the building. Such social areas tend to be largely self-regulating, but for schools, the areas should be located so that administrative staff can monitor them through large windows. A checklist of suggested items to look for when assessing the effectiveness of your school entry is attached as an appendix at the end of this chapter.

SAFETY AND SECURITY AT THE ENTRANCE

The area just past the doors of a school facility has become one of the most controversial spaces in our society during the last twenty years. Shocking, high-profile school shootings in American schools such as the Newtown, Connecticut, shooting in 2013 have led many schools to take security measures like installing metal detectors, uniformed guards, and meshed glass—the components of jails, essentially. Beyond the fear of the random shooter, urban schools are often concerned about gang violence as well. Once these security features are in place, they are rarely removed. Yet the truth is, extreme violence in schools is statistically rare, whereas ongoing negative experiences like bullying are far more prevalent.[2] Although it's easy to understand the concern of the adults who instigate these security devices, it's also important to assess how the devices might affect members of the school community that must use these facilities daily. What is the best way to make school entries safe without sacrificing designs that nurture students and promote positive social behavior?

The main entry area is the most critical checkpoint to monitor access to the school building, but the techniques used and the design of the space need not resemble those of a prison. Even more-discrete forms of electronic monitoring may not be the best application for school security. Smart cards and video surveillance systems, with their implied distrust of the student body, are the antithesis of welcoming.

The very best way to provide for security and safety in a school is the concept of "eyes on the street," or passive human observation.[3] Design features that enable passive surveillance are open commons, transparent partitions, low walls, and a variety of lighting especially at entrances. While schools typically have the administration block near the entrance, or someone at a desk in the front, they have less adult presence than they could; the person at the desk might have to leave to assist someone, or the few people in admin with the view of the front could be distracted by their work. Administration offices have the best chance for strong passive surveillance when the majority of the inhabitants can look up from their work and observe the entrance or commons. Such an arrangement can be facilitated by the use of longer, transparent walls. Because crime rates peak in schools at ages thirteen to fifteen, passive supervision at middle schools is especially important.[4] At Meadowdale Middle School, outside Seattle, the design of the entrance funnels people past the glass walls of the admin office, then into a school commons.

Another key to successful passive supervision is sight lines, or the elimination of obstacles to views in the school, particularly at the entrance. Ed Peterson, school superintendent of the Meadowdale School District, remarks that "it's the easiest school in the district to supervise; even one person can do it. I can stand here in the commons and see most of the school from this one vantage point." The inclusion of sight lines doesn't mean the space needs to be boring or lack furnishings. Rather, it means that there are always adult eyes monitoring every space and providing social guidance when needed. This method not only protects the school from outside dangers, but is also a strong deterrent to bullying and other lower-level threats to student well-being.

At the smaller Jackson Elementary School in Medford, Oregon, administrators behind the cornered glass wall easily monitor a foyer just inside the entrance; they also have a clear view of the commons beyond. Sliding glass panels allow the administrators to greet and guide school visitors as well. The offices behind have window walls that directly view the overhang space just outside the door and the area where the buses let the students off. When entries are designed for passive supervision, it becomes easy for an administrator or a parent volunteer to greet any visitor with a friendly "Welcome to our school," and "Can I help you find your way?"

During a visit to Cristo Rey Jesuit High School in Minneapolis, I arrived at the beginning of the school day in October. The school is located in a lower-income neighborhood, and every student has a business internship position he or she works at daily, so there's lots of coming and going there. In addition, the school shares some of its gym and theater with the Colin Powell Community Center later in the day. As I moved toward the entrance, a short line of students was forming and then moving into the school, but the reason wasn't a metal detector. A receiving line comprising the school principal and four or five teachers stood just inside the door, greeting students by name and shaking their hands. By entering each student's personal zone respectfully, the adults in the school community forged a connection with the students.

For students, beginning the day with a positive social experience forms a feeling of personal identification with the school and prepares them for a better learning experience. Ironically, such simple measures are more likely to help prevent repeat incidents of school violence than impersonal and expensive security systems because the social approach addresses the problem at its cause: student alienation. Common sense would suggest that students who feel welcomed and cared for by adults in a school are less likely to lash out violently than students who are invisible in an anonymous crowd in an institutional setting.

THE HEART OF SCHOOL AND A POSITIVE SOCIAL CLIMATE

After being greeted, a visitor to a school finds himself or herself in a space where both visitors and students usually pause; a visitor might wait here for an appointment, and students gather here before the school day begins. Because this space is where people spend the most time upon entering the school building, it's important to consider the area both architecturally and in terms of furnishings and other elements like signage and student display. As the centering point between the learning communities and various academic zones, this space can be referred to as the *heart of school*. Let's consider the elements that create a positive environment in this centering area.

Lighting

The desire for natural light and warm tones inside the entrance is nearly always mentioned during my interactions with school communities, particularly in northern climates. Window walls combined with the use of wood can provide an inviting environment that's suitable for a variety of climates. As this space is meant to be relatively stimulating, colors from the warmer spectrum are appropriate for all but the hottest parts of the world, where whites and blues offer visual relief from desert ochers or dense green vegetation. Color choices can also be drawn from the local culture. Lighting should enhance the color choices. Fixtures that are varied offer the best kind of artificial light for the heart of school; track fixtures for student display, wall washes, linear directional and low-voltage light combine to enhance the space far better than the grid of uniform fluorescent lighting so often encountered in the public buildings of the last century.[5]

Acoustics

Sound must be carefully regulated, particularly in larger common spaces, since too much noise can inhibit social interaction.[6] You can modulate sound with changes in ceiling and floor height and with ceiling acoustical panels, upholstered walls, and the judicious use of carpeting. Creating niches for individual or small-group study also inhibits sound "bounce" and amplification that can happen with long, straight walls. The amplification from long school corridors full of metal lockers is probably a distinct memory for anyone who attended a traditional high school. The use of soft furnishings and curtain panels can also help keep this busy, multiuse area stimulating rather than stressful.

Seating

Both visitors and students will benefit from being able to choose from a variety of seating, at different heights; the use of both built-in and movable furnishings makes the space more agile. Long window ledges, stairs wide enough to sit on, and built-in banquettes become magnets for kids to socialize or study on. It's rarely effective to place furniture in the kind of contrived groupings prevalent in corporate lobbies or airports. As Bryan Lawson says in *The Language of Space*, "beautifully designed seats in the middle of an open space may look very sculptural, but they will remain just that—sculpture. By comparison, people will sit on any object that is well located."[7] To this end, some commons furniture should be easy to move and rearrange, so that students and adults can create configurations that are "well located" for the needs of a variety of groups and individuals.

FIGURE 2.6 **At Roosevelt Elementary School in Medford, Oregon, both soft seating and a window seat offer inviting places to read and do projects.**

It is, however, best to have the visitor waiting area configured slightly more formally than the rest of the space and located near the administration office. This more permanent seating area visually draws visitors to it with a reassuringly familiar formation. It gives them a place to retreat to and a view of the activity around them. An adjacent coffee or beverage bar is a friendly feature that can be useful for larger evening events like parent-teacher nights. This waiting area is also a good place to present images of school activity, both past and present, to inform the visitor about school culture.

Signage

Another important component in putting people at ease in an unfamiliar space, signage allows visitors, the community, and new students to navigate the building independently. If the common areas of the school are used by the community or for sporting events, then signs should point to public areas like the theater, cafeteria, athletic facilities, and conference rooms. Even school signs can provide a lesson in the learning building. A fun and inexpensive way to involve students is to have them create a school visitor map yearly, which can be printed and available in the visitors waiting area.

Signature

Elements that speak of the school's identity are not just for the outside entry. In Canada, indoor amenities like stone fireplaces, indoor gardens, and play areas are often suggested by participants in planning workshops. Used as a focal point, these signature elements can add a welcoming ambience to the space and give it structure. In warm-weather countries like Oman, water features, mosaic floors, and geometric grillwork evoke the local spirit while cooling the space. School history can be another avenue for exploring signature concepts; a stretch of wall could be a timeline, added to yearly. Choosing the items would make for an interesting schoolwide project.

Display

Student display can be a revealing form of signature, but it's important to consider authenticity when choosing pieces for display in the heart of school. Rows of fairly identical sheets from a rote assignment are simply not as compelling as a heartfelt work that marks the individuality of the student who created it. Rather than just being stuck to a wall, artwork in a school entry space should be displayed with the same honor given to the sporting trophies and photos, behind glass or carefully framed. Choices can move beyond the obvious two-dimensional posters and include science models, gardens, dioramas, and photographs of students practicing various learning modalities. Another interesting idea is to design part of an actual learning space, say, a robotics or other unique studio, with transparent walls that open to the heart of school, to showcase real-time learning as a signature element.

Technology

Electronic display is another outlet for creative student work like videos and animation, which brings us to the presence of technology in the entry and central commons. The all-school commons, after all, should also be a learning space and needs Wi-Fi so that students can work there independently. Some standing-height desktop computers are also appropriate to have in this space since they allow for quick referral and research without the students' having to boot up laptop computers.

THE COMMUNITY COMMONS AND SOCIALIZATION

The school commons is the final segment of our journey through the school's entry areas, but there are some further interesting details and possibilities to examine before moving on to the next chapter.

Whenever I visit schools, I see students sprawled on the floor in hallways studying, groups practicing a small performance while leaning against some lockers, literally kids roaming in packs looking for somewhere to work, even in very expensive private school settings. A properly furnished school commons with a variety of niches, table sizes, soft seating, ledges, and steps can accommodate all kinds of learning modalities and socialization in a safe place under passive supervision. Indeed, even very inexpensive remodels can produce school commons through the removal of some walls and the creative use of furniture. This space can also serve as a meeting point between the school and the local community (see the sidebar "The School Commons as a Community Center").

In underserved communities, a mixed-use facility can stabilize the neighborhood and cluster helpful agencies in one place. This holistic approach was utilized during the planning phase of the North Central Shared Facility in Regina, Saskatchewan. The project integrates a grade 8–12 secondary school, community center, health clinic, grocery store, police station, garden center, café, and First Nations center in a single facility along an indoor "street." Integrated programming in the school provides students with internships and mentoring from police officers and tribal elders, while leveraging the economy and efficiency of one highly sustainable facility.

The Jackson and Roosevelt schools in Medford, Oregon, take a similar but less extensive school-as-community-resource vein. Several public meeting rooms are situated adjacent to the schools' central commons, while the student learning communities are beyond this agile space. During the day, volunteers from groups like the Grandparent Reading Program can tutor students one-on-one or in small groups in the commons; this kind of intervention is valuable in a multicultural neighborhood where kids from immigrant families often need help with language skills. In the evening, the atriums and meeting rooms can be used by the neighborhood for musical performances and adult education. Thus the school forms a partnership with the community—a partnership that goes beyond simply using the same spaces. As Phil Long, superintendent of district schools, says, "I like the way that the space can be transformed depending on the audience, where

THE SCHOOL COMMONS
AS A COMMUNITY CENTER

There are many places where the school building is the heart of the community. In schools like these, commons areas can expand to encompass more amenities, acting as a positive draw for the surrounding neighborhood. Examples include:

- Cafés
- Performance spaces
- Health services
- Libraries
- Daycares

- Gymnasiums
- Meeting rooms
- Media theaters
- Workout facilities
- Swimming pools

The concept of shared community assets can work both ways; students can use outside amenities for learning, or the school can become the focus of local public life.

it can go from a place for adult discourse to a child-centered space. There's nothing more thrilling than when you're here in the morning and they're doing an all-school assembly, with the young kids down below and the older ones up on level two, the whole school community participating as a group."

These examples demonstrate that the school commons can integrate the surrounding community at any scale that makes sense for a school. Neighborhoods that need more help because their people are economically challenged or new to the country can benefit by having services close by and integrated. Wealthier areas with many community assets might use the commons as a connecting point where students move out to an internship or study at a local college library. This connection needs to go beyond simply shared usage to a true partnership of meaningful relationships between all entities, and the entry transition must help sustain these important human interactions.

FIGURE 2.7 An attractive commons area at Jackson Elementary School in Medford, Oregon, is directly accessible from the main entry. This day-lit space features many locations for reading, working with computers, and team collaboration. It is also an excellent venue for after-hours parent and community meetings.

SMALLER COMMONS SPACES: ENTRIES TO LEARNING COMMUNITIES

Commons can also be created throughout the school on a smaller scale. Often they serve as entries to individual learning communities. These areas are different from the main school entry but no less important.

Let's look at the learning commons area in the temporary high school at the International School of Brussels to see exactly why agility makes the area so successful. Teachers and students appreciate that they can choose where they want to sit to work, and many gravitate to the windows for the sunlight and vistas. One particular teacher has a preferred place at the long table and rarely uses her designated office space. Many of the students enjoy lounging on the soft seating for small group meetings, and all of them can gather there for a presentation from a guest lecturer. The entire room full of furnishings, including the lockers, can be easily rearranged into these configurations to allow teachers and students to experiment with different forms of learning. Pilot projects like this one at ISB offer opportunities for a school to try out and perfect new learning environments in a relatively small space without a large capital outlay.

On an even smaller scale, the teachers of Hartland-Lakeside School District in Wisconsin began to change their teaching, so they decided to open up some classrooms into commons areas. Therese Jilek, director of instruction and technology, explains: "Teachers realized that differentiated methods and changing their learning expectations for students required an environment that was radically different than rows or groups of desks. Creating comfortable spaces that reflected the world outside of the classroom began to take shape."[8] As these teachers realized they were becoming facilitators of learning rather than dispensers, they knew they needed more-agile spaces, but they didn't have much of a budget to work with, so they got creative. Low tables with casters, beanbags, rocker stools, and thick rugs allow active students to move and more relaxed kids to lounge and read. Deals were made with local suppliers to keep costs low. This quote from a third-grader shows how well they succeeded: "My desk used to feel like my prison. I used to sit in school and think about being at home where I could get comfortable. Now, I'm just as comfortable at school as I am at home."[9]

Obviously, this kid is more ready to learn now than he was before. Increasing commons areas in schools on any scale provides students with more opportunities to learn in a way that best suits them personally.

APPENDIX (CHAPTER 2): WELCOMING ENTRY CHECKLIST

Use this checklist to score your school's entries for each feature, and then comment on how the entries might be improved.

Description			Comments
Entry has appropriate scaled, covered canopy to protect people from sun and rain while they wait for, meet, and greet friends and others outside main entrance and entrance to each school.	√ Yes	√ No	
Younger and older students enter site from different entrances.	√ Yes	√ No	
Parents of the youngest children are able to walk their child to class or some common receiving area.	√ Yes	√ No	
Past security, there is welcoming signage that is clearly visible.	√ Yes	√ No	
Adults in administrative areas are able to visually supervise student entrances to buildings.	√ Yes	√ No	
Aesthetic and easy-to-read signage clearly directs all visitors to appropriate destination	√ Yes	√ No	
A signature element announcing the school's ethos is clearly visible by the main ceremonial entrance to the school.	√ Yes	√ No	
The walk to each school entry is pleasant and sheltered from the sun and has visual access to green areas.	√ Yes	√ No	
Administrative areas have transparency so that staff or volunteers can visually monitor people entering the building.	√ Yes	√ No	

Description			Comments
Each visitor is immediately greeted by someone as he or she enters the building.	√ Yes	√ No	
There are display boards integrally designed on wall surfaces plus places to display 3-D student projects at the main entrance and at each secondary entrance.	√ Yes	√ No	
Special display area has been set aside for school history.	√ Yes	√ No	
Comfortable and adequate seating is available for visitors.	√ Yes	√ No	
Welcoming signage directs parents and others in the community to dedicated community meeting and conferencing space, with appropriate furnishings and access to beverages.	√ Yes	√ No	
There is a community gathering and waiting area with comfortable chairs in an acoustically controlled environment.	√ Yes	√ No	
Area has a small self-service café cart outside the office or a school café open to parents for morning and afternoon coffee, tea, and snacks.	√ Yes	√ No	
Area is extremely well lit with daylight and appropriate artificial light.	√ Yes	√ No	
A student drop-off area near the entry works well in the mornings and evenings without clogging traffic.	√ Yes	√ No	

CHAPTER THREE

Capturing More Space for Learning

Reconfiguring Classrooms and Hallways

THE CLASSROOM IS an obvious place to start when we are talking about redesigning schools—but why hallways? Why are these two spaces, one designed for learning and the other intended to be a utilitarian space, lumped together in one chapter? The short answer to this question is that in a vast majority of schools in the United States, classrooms are aligned along hallways. This arrangement signifies a particular philosophy of school design—one I have characterized earlier as the cells-and-bells model. The model is designed to efficiently move students from one "cell" (classroom) to another identical cell when the bell rings. A different system, organized around student-centered learning instead of teacher-centered learning, will require a different architectural response. By eliminating the rigid separation that now exists between classrooms and hallways, much if not all the space previously set aside for hallways will become usable for teaching and learning, and the classrooms themselves can be configured in much more flexible ways.

This chapter does not propose one magic solution to replace the traditional classroom and hallway design. Nor does it suggest that every school will be

FIGURE 3.1 This commons area at the P. K. Yonge Developmental Research School at the University of Florida in Gainesville shows how eliminating hallways from school designs creates more learning space per square foot.

prepared to do away altogether with classrooms and hallways. Instead, I provide concrete solutions that any school can adopt, no matter where it is in its transformation. The journey starts with modest improvements to the traditional model, in which individual classrooms are converted into learning studios (i.e., redesigned classrooms, which will be discussed in detail later in the chapter). From learning studios, we move on to the creation of learning suites, where two or more classrooms are combined to enable teachers to work collaboratively. The chapter ends with a complete reconfiguration of the whole classroom-hallway arrangement to create new-paradigm learning communities. But in the meantime, the sidebar "Do Now: An Exercise in Imagination" provides specific, low-cost ideas that teachers can start to implement immediately.

DO NOW: AN EXERCISE IN IMAGINATION

Even if you have very little or no money for renovations, there is hope. The most important change you can make is to start thinking of the space that used to be your classroom as your learning studio. This change is more than a semantic distinction. The word *room* suggests a place that is very much contained and closed to the spaces around it. *Studio*, on the other hand, suggests a space that is full of opportunity—an artist's studio contains all the materials he or she needs to practice with, and it invites the outside world in. The inspiration of natural life or city life is embraced in a studio. Imagine your classroom as a learning studio—a space that contains many inspirations for learning, that invites authentic learning opportunities, and that relates strongly to its surroundings.

Here are ten suggestions for getting started:

- *Discard the mental model:* Remember that the classroom "box" exists not only as a physical place but as a mental one as well. Start by renaming the classroom—call it your *learning studio*, for all the reasons discussed in this chapter.
- *Assign a group project:* Have your students work with the research (try http://designshare.com) to figure out an alternative way to furnish the box.
- *Develop an "activities matrix":* Decide which of the twenty modalities of learning can be reasonably accommodated in the spaces previously used as classrooms.
- *Repeat this mantra: "soft is good":* Make sure that the plan includes soft seating (a couch, upholstered chairs, cushions, and beanbags are all worth considering).
- *Test the design:* Using templates for furniture, test the different ways in which the room can be arranged to facilitate different modes of learning.
- *Raise funds, get it used, and try home improvement stores:* Develop and implement a plan to raise money for new furniture or (better still) approach local businesses or corporations for donations of their used furniture that matches your desired plan. Ask your local home and office improvement stores for donations of paint and equipment to build shelves, display boards, windowsills, and so on.
- *Make it green:* Use this project as a conscious exercise in environmental responsibility by choosing indigenous materials, connecting with the outdoors and nature, and expending minimal resources.
- *Build it yourself:* If students build it, they will love it and take care of it.
- *Take down some walls:* If you have a bit of renovation money, take down some walls to facilitate team teaching, create social spaces, and break out of corridors.
- *Change your practice:* Change your teaching and learning practices to take advantage of what you have created.

CLASSROOMS AND HALLWAYS AS SINGLE-PURPOSE SPACES

The design of classrooms is flawed in its ability to accommodate activities that allow children to be creative and agile learners. Typical classroom design is based on the erroneous assumption that efficient delivery of content is the same as effective learning. Most classrooms are best adapted to a single mode of instruction—lecturing from the front of the room—and reinforce the norm that each teacher works in isolation behind the closed door of his or her own room.

As the primary place for student learning, the classroom does not withstand the scrutiny of scientific research. Environmental scientists have published dozens of studies that show a close correlation between human productivity and space design.[1] This research clearly demonstrates that students and teachers do better when they have variety, flexibility, and comfort in their environment—the very qualities that classrooms lack.

Hallways, like most traditional classrooms, are single-purpose spaces. Even more problematic, they remain unused for a majority of the school day. Their lack of versatility and their scarce use combine to make hallways very inefficient. Beyond that, hallways are an obvious example of dysfunctional design because they are areas that encourage negative behaviors like bullying and vandalism.[2]

What if hallways could be turned into a space used for teaching and learning throughout the day? Not only would this change allow schools to break out of the trap of conventional classroom design, but it would almost magically add nearly 20 to 30 percent more usable space to the average school!

THE FOUR PRIMORDIAL LEARNING METAPHORS

A well-designed space will allow students to experience four overarching learning modes—described by David Thornburg as "primordial learning metaphors": *campfire* (learning from an expert), *watering hole* (learning from peers), *cave* (learning from introspection), and *life* (learning by doing). One of the founding members of the Xerox Palo Alto Research Center, Thornburg is an award-winning futurist, author, and PBS commentator who has been active in the field of education since the late 1970s. He believes that real learning only occurs when learners have an opportunity to cycle through most or all of these four modes on a regular basis. In a seminal article, "Campfires in Cyberspace," and a book of the same title, he contrasted a very tedious conference he had attended—a meeting filled with expert speakers (campfire mode)—with another conference, which offered participants

FIGURE 3.2 *Before:* A vast majority of schools follow this cells-and-bells arrangement of classrooms situated along a double-loaded corridor lined with student lockers. This particular hallway at Hillel Academy of Tampa, Florida, can boast of some limited natural light and views to the outside—features that are absent in a majority of the school designs. This hallway takes up nearly 30 percent of the total space in this wing of the school—space that lies fallow during most of the school day and is thus largely wasted.

FIGURE 3.3 *After:* This photo shows the same Hillel Academy hallway featured in the cells-and-bells photo above. The renovated space is now part of a small learning community. Notice the variety of social and working areas created through the use of furnishings. Note also that the glass openings to the adjacent classrooms (which were in turn converted to learning studios) bring in more daylight and brighten the space. This renovation was completed for a small fraction of what school districts normally spend on school facilities renovations.

The Four Learning Metaphors, Illustrated

FIGURE 3.4 *Cave* space for introspective learning at Jackson Elementary School in Medford, Oregon.

FIGURE 3.5 *Campfire* space for learning in a group at P. K. Yonge School.

FIGURE 3.6 *Watering hole* space for casual peer learning at Cristo Rey Jesuit High School in Minneapolis.

FIGURE 3.7 Learning from *life* through real-world experiences at Jackson Elementary School.

frequent breaks to network (watering hole mode) or just take a long walk along the beach (cave) and work together to solve problems (life). He suggested that the latter conference was far more effective because it provided the attendees an opportunity to experience all four primordial learning modes.[3]

After reading what Thornburg had to say, I decided to apply his theory in the world of school design. Schools, like the expert-filled conference, are heavily oriented to the campfire mode of learning. Good schools must have a balance of spaces to accommodate all four modes of learning in order to allow students to fully benefit from their education. Over the past ten years, the metaphors of campfire, watering hole, cave, and life are now well recognized among architects and commonly used in school design. They can even be found in government guidelines and standards.

Today's classrooms are primarily designed for the campfire mode of learning—learning from an expert. The purpose of the classroom as a campfire space is further reinforced when all the seats are aligned so that they face the teacher at the front of the room. Given that students spend the majority of their school day in classrooms, it is extremely difficult for educators to design programs that will provide the rich mix of learning activities recommended by David Thornburg.

UNDERSTANDING MULTIPLE WAYS OF LEARNING

The Thornburg metaphors are a good starting point for understanding the need for variety in learning environments, but they do not specifically talk about learning activities that a well-designed school building should support. Architect Randall Fielding and I have identified twenty modalities of learning that can become the basis for the design of effective learning spaces (see the sidebar "Twenty Modalities of Learning").

During a typical week, students in most schools will experience many if not all the twenty modalities of learning. But simply experiencing the twenty modalities in and of themselves is not the same as getting a twenty-first-century education. Think about having a variety of ingredients in your kitchen cabinet but not being able to access them when you need them. In the same way, neither teachers nor students are able to access every modality of learning when and where it is needed. As soon as a school is "zoned" so that different learning activities happen in different parts of the school, then the seamlessness needed for students to quickly cycle between several learning activities is lost. The appendix "Best Spaces for Various

TWENTY MODALITIES OF LEARNING

1. Independent study
2. Peer-to-peer tutoring
3. One-on-one learning with teacher
4. Teacher lecture
5. Team collaboration
6. Project-based learning
7. Distance learning
8. Learning with mobile technology
9. Student presentations
10. Internet-based research
11. Roundtable discussions
12. Performance-based learning
13. Interdisciplinary study
14. Naturalist learning
15. Art-based learning
16. Social-emotional learning
17. Design-based learning
18. Storytelling
19. Team teaching and learning
20. Play- and movement-based learning

Types of Learning" at the end of this chapter shows how changing the space configuration of schools yields dramatically different teaching and learning benefits.

Classrooms are good for lectures and student presentations but don't work for most of the other modalities, like team collaboration, independent study, peer-to-peer tutoring, and so on. In most schools, you will actually see more than two modes of learning taking place in traditional classrooms, but traditional classrooms are not consciously well designed to accommodate a variety of learning activities.

For example, teachers could ask twenty-five students to sit quietly at their desks and read, and an observer could then say that all twenty-five students are "learning independently." What this observation fails to account for is that given an opportunity to pick their own type of space in which to read quietly, few children would choose their uncomfortable desk and chair as the ideal place for this activity. A well-designed school will provide a variety of areas that students could pick from, depending upon their own personal preferences for the activity in question. For this reason, I assert that traditional classrooms are "well-designed" only for two learning modalities—teacher lecture and student presentations.

FIGURE 3.8 A typical classroom in a traditional floor plan arrangement. Notice how the individual student desks and chairs are lined up in rows facing the teacher at the front of the room.

FIGURE 3.9 Contrast this image with the traditional classroom arrangement at top. The studio was transformed through the use of a variety of furnishings and student groupings, the replacement of the fixed whiteboard with a mobile one, and connections to an outdoor learning environment and to an indoor commons.

Now see what happens when you string a group of classrooms together along a double loaded corridor, the most typical arrangement found in a majority of schools in the United States. There is absolutely no change to the learning modalities count—a group of classrooms set up in a traditional fashion is suitable for the same number of learning modalities—two. In other words, there is no added educational benefit whatsoever (measured by the increase in the number of activities that students can actually do) when classrooms are grouped in this way. This result is not surprising; classrooms are placed in clusters along a hallway because of efficiency of movement and not effectiveness of learning.

FROM CLASSROOMS TO LEARNING STUDIOS

In the journey from a twentieth-century to a twenty-first-century school design, the first and simplest step is to convert classrooms into learning studios. Very simply, a *learning studio* is a classroom that is consciously redesigned to increase the number of learning modalities that can be accomplished within its four walls. In fact, the most common example of a learning studio is an early-childhood classroom. These classrooms are usually outfitted with various age-appropriate "learning centers" for different activities—say, sand and water tables, a reading area, a meeting rug, a dress-up corner, and so forth.

The three floor plans depicted in the figures show the various learning arrangements possible in the same physical space. The top floor plan is a traditional classroom configuration. The middle plan is a series of learning studios that would be suitable for middle and high school students. It is easy to see that the learning studios will permit many more teaching and learning activities than the traditional classroom. The bottom plan is an advisory model that gives every student his or her own workstation.

Learning studios for younger and older students will be designed differently because elementary-age children spend more time in their homerooms and need access to more modes of learning there, whereas older students are more mobile and have access to specialized facilities in other parts of the school that cannot be accommodated within their learning studio. In both cases, learning studios provide a much richer range of teaching and learning activities. Learning studios are better not only because they permit more modes of learning but also because they are more comfortable, more cheerful, and happier places for students. The chapter appendix, "Best Spaces for Various Types of Learning," shows that learning studios

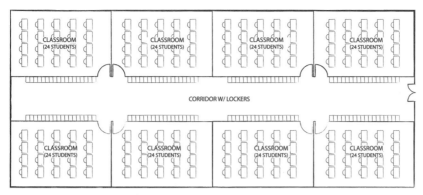

FIGURE 3.10　Typical Classrooms and Hallway Floor Plan

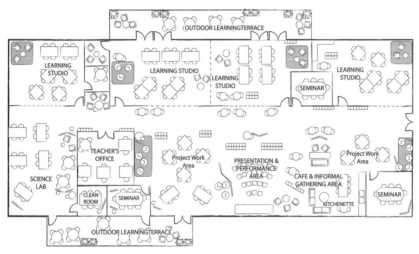

FIGURE 3.11　Transforming the Classroom-Hallway Plan into a Small Learning Community

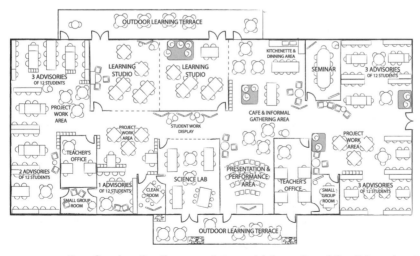

FIGURE 3.12　Transforming the Classroom into an Advisory-Based Small Learning Community

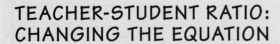

TEACHER-STUDENT RATIO: CHANGING THE EQUATION

There is a lot written about the ideal teacher-student ratio for public schools. Schools that are set up in a traditional classroom arrangement have no flexibility in the teacher-student ratio, which is fixed by the number of students in any given classroom. School spaces that are configured according to the small learning center (SLC) model have an advantage in this regard. As the chart shows, SLC-based schools can continuously adjust teacher-student ratios according to the learning activity.

Learning Modality	Acceptable Teacher-Student Ratio	Explanation
Teacher lecture	1:10 to 1:150 or greater*	One lecturer can address a larger number of students almost as effectively a smaller number. For example, an expert who visits the school may address an entire SLC or the whole student body in an auditorium.
Independent study, Internet-based research, peer-to-peer tutoring, team collaboration	0:25	In the modes of learning identified, the teacher within the SLC can remain on the sidelines or be working with another group of students, because all these activities are student directed.
One-on-one learning with teacher	1:1	By reducing the need for teachers to be actively "teaching" while students are in self-directed mode, and with the assurance that colleagues are watching other students, individual teachers in SLCs can be freed up to give one-on-one attention to students who need it.
Small group instruction	1:5	One teacher can be very effective working with a small group of about five students.
Roundtable discussions	1:15	One teacher and fifteen students can be at a conference or round table for group discussion and "Socratic"-style instruction.

*Any ratio from 1:10 to 1:150 (the size of an SLC) to one teacher for the entire school.

In an SLC, where a group of teachers is responsible for a group of students, the teacher-student ratio can constantly vary throughout the school day without the need to hire any more teachers. Even with an increased number of students on a per-teacher basis, individual students who need it will get more attention from teachers. In other words, a teacher-student ratio of 1 to 25 in an SLC model may be equivalent to a ratio of 1 to 20 in a classroom model. For school districts, the financial ramifications of this approach are huge.

are well designed for between five and seven modalities of learning—significantly more than traditional classrooms, which are suitable for only two modalities.

FROM LEARNING STUDIOS TO LEARNING SUITES

Learning suites are created when two or more learning studios are combined by the opening up of a wall between studios by way of a simple opening, sliding door, or movable wall. While the removal of a barrier is a relatively small architectural change, it has a major impact on teaching and learning. Suddenly, teachers are no longer isolated with a defined group of students. The educators can work collaboratively and have more opportunities to rearrange student groups, provide one-to-one help for students who need it, work in block schedules, create interdisciplinary projects, share space to increase learning opportunities because both studios don't have to be designed identically, and create mixed-age groupings.

Even with a traditional school staffing structure that allocates twenty-five students to one teacher, teachers in a suite of learning studios can work together, perhaps each with a different purpose, to create a wider range of learning opportunities (see the sidebar "Teacher-Student Ratio: Changing the Equation.")[4] Learning suites are suitable for ten modalities of learning, including one-on-one learning with the teacher, peer-to-peer tutoring, and team teaching and learning (see chapter appendix).

FROM LEARNING SUITES TO SMALL LEARNING COMMUNITIES

This brings us to the design of small learning communities (SLC), where we start to look beyond individual classrooms and classroom pairs to the entire wing of a traditional school building.[5] We have already seen how a group of classrooms along a hallway provides no learning advantage over a single classroom. However, when the space occupied by the same group of classrooms and hallway is transformed into an SLC, the number of potential learning activities increase dramatically. Small learning communities allow nineteen of the twenty modalities of learning to be done well.

Small Learning Communities Versus Small Schools

It is important to distinguish a school based on the SLC model from the small-schools model, which was very big for several years in the United States and beyond. With grant money from influential organizations such as the Bill & Melinda Gates

FIGURE 3.13 One important advantage of a small learning community is that students can access a learning commons area like this one. The commons expands the scope of the various modes of learning beyond those that can be accomplished in learning studios. These spaces are smaller than the school commons and tend to be mostly used by the learning community members.

and Annenberg foundations, and with school systems themselves investing heavily to break down the scale of their larger schools, small schools had been poised to permanently shift the national thinking toward thinking small. However, the results of the small-schools movement were disappointing. Efforts to foster a sense of community by breaking down large high schools into smaller "schools-within-schools" did not pan out as predicted.

Unfortunately, SLCs got caught up in the failure of the small-schools movement perhaps because both were about going small. However, many so-called small schools had over 500 students and some capped out at over 1,000. These schools were considered small only insofar as they represented smaller sub-sets of the larger 3,000- to 4,000-student high schools that they were originally a part of.

From the perspective of an individual student attending one of these schools, the schools were anything but small! So it is not surprising that the anticipated benefits of smallness did not materialize.

Simply reducing school size is clearly not enough to improve student performance. However, research suggests that small school size may act as a facilitator of desirable practices such as teacher collaboration and collegiality, improved student-teacher relationships, and more personalized instruction, simply because these practices are easier to implement in smaller learning communities.[6]

There is a growing consensus among educators that SLCs should include no more than 150 students—preferably fewer. In fact, there may be a scientific basis for this limitation. In his book *The Tipping Point*, Malcolm Gladwell refers to evolutionary biology as the reason human beings have what he calls a "social-channel capacity" that limits the number of people they can effectively interact with.[7] Gladwell quotes British anthropologist Robin Dunbar, who contends that "the figure of 150 seems to represent the maximum number of individuals with whom we can have a genuinely social relationship."[8]

The Small Learning Community, by Design

The most important condition for an SLC's success lies in the word *community*. The key is to create autonomous or semiautonomous student groups so that the sense of smallness is real and doesn't seem like just another administrative gimmick. It's a prime responsibility of those who design schools to support the kind of autonomy needed for an SLC to be successful.

When architect Randall Fielding designed Harbor City International Charter School, in Duluth, Minnesota, for example, he wanted to create a place where the staff and the school's two hundred students felt connected. The self-contained distribution of elements at this school is vastly different from the typical classroom-and-corridor arrangement typical of most schools' architecture.

At Harbor City, a variety of spaces combine to create a completely autonomous learning environment. Square footage normally taken up by corridors is now devoted to student workstations and breakout areas for social learning. Soft-seating "oases" can be used not only for individual studying and collaborative learning but also for eating lunch. Though the layout seems open and capacious, this kind of approach can usually be done within the same overall space used for a traditional hallway-based plan. The significant difference is that in this kind of SLC, all the space is used for learning and student activities.

To achieve this kind of efficient design where all the space is usable space, it is important to think differently about partitions that separate one learning activity from another. Whereas traditional schools tend to use solid masonry partitions to separate learning activities, innovatively designed learning communities resort to a variety of ways to differentiate spaces. These features tend to be just as effective as walls but are less permanent and create opportunities to vary the size and ambiance of spaces to best suit the learning activity that is happening at any given time. Please see the sidebar "Smart Idea: Partitions" for some examples.

Though it's not always easy to duplicate the benefits of small schools such as Harbor City within larger schools, it is possible. The key is to avoid the fundamental mistake of the Gates-inspired small schools-within-schools, which as noted earlier, often capped out at 500 to 1,000 students. Not only do schools feel impersonal at this scale, but they are also difficult if not impossible to administer as learning communities. Effective learning communities will have no more than 150 students and up to eight teachers. At this size, the SLCs look, feel, and operate like true communities.

At the Hillel Academy of Tampa, Florida, my colleagues and I designed two learning communities—one for students in grades 2–5 and the other for students in grades 6–8. At the 1,500-student International School of Brussels (ISB), we designed the whole master plan with a view toward breaking down the school into SLCs. At ISB, each SLC is a semiautonomous unit, but students share larger elements in the school such as the auditorium, the media center, and the physical fitness facility. Bloomfield Hills High School in Michigan will be located in a renovated and expanded existing high school campus. It is designed to accommodate up to 1,650 students in eleven SLCs. In all the successful examples of SLCs mentioned here, a common theme is the need for self-contained social space, which often becomes a central and defining aspect of the new design.

Today, many schools that at first look traditional have already begun to group students into what are called advisories, rather than classrooms or homerooms. The term *advisory* can be used simply to designate a group of students who meet on a regular basis. When this idea is combined with SLCs, advisories take on a whole new meaning. Advisory-based SLCs provide individual workstations for groups of 10 to 15 students for a total of about 150 students who share common areas like a café, project areas, learning studios, seminar rooms, teacher collaboration rooms, and so on. In an advisory model, each student has his or her own workstation to support a predominantly student-centered (and often project-based) curriculum.

FIGURE 3.14 This learning studio and the one adjacent to it at the American School of Bombay are joined together using a sliding, multipanel partition. This design allows the two rooms to function together as one learning suite, at the discretion of the teachers. The partitions themselves include tack boards, whiteboards, and glass panels.

SMART IDEA: PARTITIONS

A key element of good school design is the smart use of partitions that separate spaces and functions. Whereas traditional schools tend to use permanent masonry partitions to separate spaces—and particularly classrooms, a learning building will use partitions as a way to both separate and combine spaces as needed. The photos are just a few examples of the intelligent use of partitions to change the traditional classroom paradigm to a more flexible one.

FIGURE 3.15 The same learning studio also has sliding partitions that separate it from the commons area that used to be a hallway but is now used extensively for learning. Depending on the activity and the extent to which acoustic separation is important, the teachers can keep the partition to the commons area more open or less so.

FIGURE 3.16 This glass overhead door at the new International School of Brussels high school can either be completely closed to maintain the learning studio behind it as a separate space or be completely opened for student-directed, collaborative learning activities that spill into the commons.

FIGURE 3.17 In this learning community at the P. K. Yonge School, partitions that separate spaces double as storage units. Many informal learning activities are separated by these low partitions that provide enclosure without the need to create separate rooms.

The growing move toward SLCs is an important step in the right direction for the organization, the architecture, and the spirit of tomorrow's schools.

CREATING SMALL LEARNING COMMUNITIES IN YOUR SCHOOL

For those of you contemplating more significant renovations and modernizations of existing cells-and-bells schools, I strongly recommend changing sections of the school where you have teachers isolated in individual classrooms into a learning community model.

Start by selecting a section of the school (ideally a whole wing of the building with direct connections to the outside) that you would like to convert into an SLC. It is important that you are able to accommodate the same number of students in the SLC that previously occupied the wing being converted. Pick a wing or a portion of a wing that currently houses no more than 100 students if you are creating an elementary school SLC and no more than 150 students if you are creating a middle school or high school SLC.

Utilize the educational effectiveness surveys (appendixes A and B, at the end of this book) to first evaluate the space being converted. The surveys are based on solid research and will stand up to rigorous scrutiny. Chances are that if you are dealing with a traditional building layout, your space will initially score very low on this survey—most probably in the "inadequate" category. An evaluation of your space before you begin any conversion is important because it provides a benchmark against which you can objectively evaluate the same space after it has been converted. Some stakeholders will probably question what they consider a fairly radical change from the familiar educational model. The survey score, which is guaranteed to improve substantially if the conversion to an SLC is done correctly, will reassure both skeptics and supporters.

ENSURING A SUCCESSFUL CONVERSION TO A SMALL LEARNING COMMUNITY

In the introduction, I discussed how four design principles need to be implemented so that the learning environment can support the six twenty-first-century educational strategies: student-centered learning; teacher collaboration; positive school climate; technology integration; flexible scheduling; and connection to the environment, community, and global network.

An SLC is the ideal vehicle for implementing the four design principles. However, this must be done consciously so that the full educational benefits of SLCs can be realized. Carefully study the criteria noted below, and ensure that your design team is complying with each item on the list.

- *Be welcoming (safe, nurturing, encouraging good citizenship):* An SLC should be designed so that it feels like a welcoming place. This begins at the entrance to the SLC. Ideally, the commons area of the SLC also serves as its entrance. This area is lively, colorful, and comfortable and makes a good first impression for visitors. The feeling of welcome has to go beyond entrances and must spread to the areas that students occupy throughout the school day. The idea is to create colorful, comfortable, and personalized settings where students feel respected and taken care of. How students behave in school has a lot to do with the hidden messages that the building sends. The designer has great influence in setting up the environment so that it feels welcoming.

- *Be versatile (agile and personalized):* The SLC should be an agile environment in that it has a variety of spaces to start with—which allows multiple forms of learning to happen simultaneously. Beyond that, areas within the community should be easy to reconfigure as needed. The SLC, through its rich variety of spaces and ambiances, should also cater to the individual needs of different students and thus feel more personal and less institutional.

- *Support varying and specific learning activities:* Make sure your SLC is designed to have some sections dedicated to specific learning activities. For example, there may be a Da Vinci studio set up specifically for hands-on and messy activities (see chapter 4), a quiet reading nook, or a small group room that will accommodate up to five people. And then, the SLC will include areas like outdoor terraces and a large commons space that can be easily reconfigured for a variety of activities. In many cases, the commons can be made larger or smaller by opening up adjacent rooms with sliding glass doors, or "garage doors." This mix of dedicated spaces and reconfigurable spaces is what make SLCs respond effectively to the changing needs of teachers and learners. Thus, a school building set up as a series of SLCs will function as a true learning building. Each SLC in your school should also support the implementation of flexible scheduling, as timing becomes less about the control of student behavior and more responsive to the needs of more meaningful learning experiences.[9]

- *Send positive messages:* Understand that the SLCs you create are characterized as much by what they are not as by what they are. They are not institutional

[handwritten margin note: How will EBD students respond to/ act within these spaces?]

spaces, they are not impersonal spaces, and they are not set up exclusively for teacher-directed learning. These factors, taken together, send positive signals to students about being valued members of a community. Beyond that, the very setup of the SLC, where a few caring adults can jointly contribute to the well-being of every student in that community, creates a positive climate. In such a positive environment, students are far more likely to exhibit positive behaviors, which in turn will lead to better discipline and better learning outcomes.

APPENDIX (CHAPTER 3):
BEST SPACES FOR VARIOUS TYPES OF LEARNING

Learning Modality	Suitable School Space					
	Single classroom	*Group of classrooms along hallway*	*Single learning studio for older students*	*Single learning studio for younger children*	*Learning suite (combination of learning studios)*	*Small learning community*
1. Independent study						√
2. Peer-to-peer tutoring					√	√
3. One-on-one learning with teacher					√	√
4. Teacher lecture	√	√	√	√	√	√
5. Team collaboration			√	√	√	√
6. Project-based learning						√
7. Distance learning						√
8. Learning with mobile technology			√	√	√	√
9. Student presentations	√	√	√	√	√	√
10. Internet-based research			√	√	√	√
11. Roundtable discussions						√
12. Performance-based learning						√
13. Interdisciplinary study				√	√	√
14. Naturalist learning						√
15. Art-based learning						√
16. Social-emotional learning					√	√
17. Design-based learning						√

Learning Modality	Suitable School Space					
	Single classroom	*Group of classrooms along hallway*	*Single learning studio for older students*	*Single learning studio for younger children*	*Learning suite (combination of learning studios)*	*Small learning community*
18. Storytelling				√		√
19. Team teaching and learning					√	√
20. Play- and movement-based learning						
Total number of modalities that the space will accommodate well	2	2	5	7	10	19

CHAPTER FOUR

Integrated Learning Areas

Labs, Studios, and Do-It-Yourself Spaces

WHAT CAN SCHOOL laboratories learn from garages? The typical American home garage is a perfect analogy for a hands-on learning center in school. The garage with its basic finishes and raw floor invites hands-on project work and experimentation to happen without fear of damage. Tools and supplies hang on the walls in sight and are easily accessible. There is adequate storage for supplies, a sturdy workbench, water and utility access, and an open floor space to support all sorts of activities. Not to mention a large garage door connecting the indoor space to the outdoors, allowing large objects to be moved in and out with ease. The driveway allows for project work to expand if needed while offering great ventilation and daylight. You can also picture music playing in the background and the buzz and satisfying feel of DIY (do it yourself) accomplishments. The garage is a symbol of DIY, an all-purpose space and a great metaphor for designing space that supports self-directed, satisfying, confidence-building, hands on learning.

Why can't school laboratories be more like this? In this chapter, we'll look at multiuse learning spaces—labs, studios, and other DIY work areas—and discover how they can be reconfigured for maximum flexibility and student-centered

FIGURE 4.1   **A garage-like space at the Lake Country School in Minneapolis.**

learning. The sidebar "Essential Qualities of a Good Lab Space" describes some of the features that encourage an effective learning experience.

WHY TRADITIONAL LABS NEED SOME RETHINKING

Traditional school buildings were designed as places that facilitated the "efficient" transfer of information from teacher to student. Learning itself was measured by how much of the information communicated by teachers was actually retained by students. Today, with the proliferation of the Internet and the various devices that connect to it, information itself is an abundant resource, easily accessed by students. As schools begin to recognize that their primary reason for existence is no longer the delivery of static content, they are freed up to focus on a model based more on skills. Of course, a skills-based model of school will look very

ESSENTIAL QUALITIES OF A GOOD LAB SPACE

The useful features of a good garage are the same ones to remember when you are planning school laboratories. You will notice many similarities between this list and the list for a Da Vinci studio:

- Raw floor—one that people are not afraid to ruin
- Tools and supplies in sight and accessible
- Storage—some open to view and some closed
- Large overhead doors for moving large items
- Sturdy workbench
- Open floor space
- Driveway, which acts as an outdoor project yard for spreading out when needed
- Water and utility access
- An opening to outdoors
- Ventilation and daylight
- Proximity or connection to living and relaxing zones

different from the content-focused schools of the past. From a design standpoint, it means schools will need to accommodate more opportunities for hands-on learning throughout the school building.

Several worldwide organizations and initiatives have highlighted that for the successful development of the key skills and competencies of the twenty-first century, learners need to be involved in project-based, hands-on, problem-solving, and applied-knowledge work. Inspiration for alternative learning spaces can come from many cultures (e.g., see the sidebar "Smart Ideas: Kivas"). Ideally, students should come to school for the things they can't do as easily at home or elsewhere.[12] That means schools and, by extension, school facilities, should provide the means and the resources to support "new" types of learning, where students can apply theory to real-world scenarios while interacting with peers and under the tutelage of teachers who serve as mentors and coaches. We recognize such places as *labs*.

SMART IDEA: KIVAS

The term *kiva* is derived from community gathering spaces that are partly underground in Pueblo Indian villages. Schools also need a version of the kiva, that is, a space that encourages small and large groups to congregate. A kiva is a highly versatile space. It can function very much like a formal auditorium accommodating a relatively large group of students. However, the advantage of a kiva is that, unlike the auditorium, it can also function as a place where smaller groups of students can gather, work, socialize, and collaborate. In fact, it can also support distance learning, peer tutoring, and independent study.

FIGURE 4.2 This kiva at Ipswich High School in Massachusetts is a versatile space that permits a variety of informal and formal teaching and learning activities. It provides a great deal of functionality to this commons area without the need for either loose or fixed furnishings.

FIGURE 4.3 Here is a different kind of kiva space that separates two levels in the new high school at the International School of Brussels. This kind of stepped seating provides far greater flexibility for informal gatherings than does traditional auditorium seating.

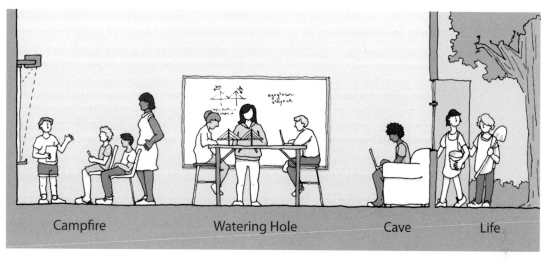

FIGURE 4.4　The Four Primordial Learning Metaphors

Whereas labs dedicated mostly to science education historically represented a small portion of the traditional school day, tomorrow's schools will see an increase in lab-like studios that support all kinds of project-based learning.

Merriam-Webster broadly defines *laboratory* as "a place providing opportunity for experimentation, observation, or practice in a field of study."[3] Note that this definition is far broader than the way the term is interpreted in traditional schools. A space equipped to provide many opportunities for experimentation, observation, or practice in a field is the quintessential definition of a real-life learning environment and will work well across all disciplines. For the purposes of this chapter, we will focus on the term *labs* with the understanding that the term has a much broader context here than encountered in a traditional school.

Let's look back at David Thornburg's four primordial learning metaphors mentioned in chapter 3: campfire (learning from an expert), watering hole (learning from peers), cave (learning from introspection), and life (learning by doing). The life metaphor is often overlooked in the design of schools, even though learning by doing is the process that completes the cycle of learning and is where theory is translated into practice. That is not to say that life is more important than the other three metaphors—all four are needed for a balanced education.

This chapter will look at the application of life learning principles schoolwide as well as in discipline-specific spaces. We will look at traditional laboratories such as science and computer labs, then look at how labs can become more interdisciplinary while expanding the range of activities they will support. Examples envisioned here include the following integrated learning areas:

- The Da Vinci studio, which serves the arts and sciences equally well
- The espresso studio
- The maker lab
- The Jamie Oliver studio
- The black-box theater

As we look at each type of learning area, we will see how the six strategies for accomplishing the twenty-first-century education goals discussed in chapter 1 are supported and how the four accompanying design principles can be implemented.

SCIENCE LABS

Science education is essential for developing the core competencies identified for learners in the twenty-first century—including research, innovation, critical thinking, experimentation, and technological innovation skills.[4] But the teaching in traditional science labs doesn't always support these goals. One recent study of student laboratory experiences concluded that the learning experience provided in American high school labs is "very poor" and fails to meet the criteria of an effective science laboratory experience. These criteria include:

- Enhancing mastery of subject matter
- Developing scientific reasoning
- Understanding the complexity and ambiguity of empirical work
- Developing practical skills
- Understanding of the nature of science
- Cultivating interest in science and interest in learning science
- Developing teamwork abilities[5]

Educators understand that science education must improve to meet the aforementioned criteria for excellence. However, the new pedagogies and learning modalities that would be in play in a modern science lab are simply impossible to deliver in a traditional science laboratory. For starters, a school lab assumes that only a limited range of practical activities associated with physics, biology, or chemistry will ever happen there. Traditional labs have very little workspace for anything else since much of the lab table is taken up with connections to services like water, gas, and electricity. The space problem is compounded when the room is crowded with too much furniture, which thereby limits opportunities to work on the floor. The crowding immediately rules out activities like building a robotic car or the scale model of a suspension bridge or sewing circuit boards into clothing.

Beyond these extensions of the regular science curriculum—tasks that would be difficult, if not impossible to do in a traditional science lab—the very idea of a lab is problematic. In the real world, scientists work in a variety of environments doing activities such as independent research, working on team projects, engaging in debates in social settings, and interacting via technology with colleagues in other parts of the world. In a highly interdisciplinary world, many so-called science projects also connect strongly with other fields, so it is important for science teachers to collaborate with teachers in other subject areas. However, the traditional science lab does not consider any of these modern needs. As a result, the educational model (what can be, and is, taught to students) is limited and includes

DISTRIBUTED TECHNOLOGY

Even though this chapter specifically addresses the design of labs, we must also consider the proper way to deploy technology in schools. When technology is done right, its easy availability (students have access to technology when it is needed and where it is needed) can make the whole school lab-like. Decentralized and dispersed technology allows for a variety of learning opportunities that would be impossible if computers were all locked up in a computer lab. We have long known the advantages of mobile computing devices that go wherever students are. Today, with the steep drop in computer prices, it makes even more sense for computers to be ubiquitously available to students in school.

What's more, today's proliferation of Internet-connected tablets and smartphones allows students ever greater freedom and flexibility when it comes to anytime, anywhere connectivity to content, resources, teachers, and each other. Entire schools thus become active labs, at least in terms of technology use.

only elements that can actually work in a traditional physical setting. In other words, the lack of twenty-first-century learning environments means the lack of a suitable science curriculum, and the lack of such a curriculum means the lack of demand for twenty-first-century educational environments. The sidebar "Distributed Technology" further discusses how inexpensive technology can widen a school's educational opportunities.

On average, students enrolled in science classes spend about one class period per week in laboratory investigations such as observing and comparing different cell types under a microscope in biology class.[6] These predetermined experiments require all students to do the same thing at the same time and in the same way to find the same solution. Again, the factory model of the traditional cells-and-bells classroom is at work here. In a learning building, the school laboratory becomes a place of real experimentation and hands-on, student-initiated, project-based learning across multiple disciplines. A great example of this kind of learning is evident at MIT's Media Lab, which permits a wide range of activities limited only by a student's imagination. While I do not expect that schools will be able to afford the level of facilities provided by MIT, they can surely learn some lessons about designing spaces that are not inherently limiting with regard to what kinds of activities and experiments can happen there. The idea is to provide a learning environment in which students will have more access to applied knowledge, experimentation, and hands-on learning, both in science education and across other subjects than they would in a traditional science lab. This change would, of course, require a change in curriculum, and in many schools, these curricular and pedagogical changes are happening, but because of the limits of the physical spaces and furniture, these new approaches are constrained by what the physical environment can support.

The goal of the learning building is to take what industry, academic experts, and researchers say are best practices for teaching and learning science knowledge and skills and create the conditions that can best support these practices. All too typically, laboratory experiences tend to be disconnected from the daily flow of science classes.[7] This isolates the application and hands-on types of learning from the day-to-day science curriculum. Ideally, labs should support both the instructional and the hands-on learning needs of a good science curriculum. To do this, however, you must define a good science curriculum—one that would not be constrained by the limits of what existing science labs will allow.

Susan Singer and her colleagues suggest that the space, furnishings, and equipment for science labs be flexible and combine the furnishings of traditional labs

DO NOW: MAKING LABS COST-EFFECTIVE

Consider these three ways to improve the cost-effectiveness of labs in schools:

Forget the class sets: Traditionally, science (and computer) labs are fitted out with class sets of supplies, tools, and equipment. Instead of spending the entire lab equipment budget on class sets of the same piece of equipment, purchase a variety of tools and supplies to facilitate different types of learning and activities in the same space.

Build industry partnerships: Another cost-saving strategy is to build relationships with community and industry partners. More often than not, either the highly specialized equipment that schools are able to purchase will go quickly out of date or the teaching staff will not be able to effectively teach the use of equipment without extensive and expensive training. It is more cost-effective and perhaps more learning-effective to partner with industry to run workshops either in or out of school with state-of-the-art equipment and expert technicians.

Share furniture, equipment, and space across all disciplines: The third strategy to increase the cost-effectiveness of labs is to consider the multidisciplinary use of furniture and equipment. This multidisciplinary approach is seen in the four alternative laboratory models presented in this chapter: the Da Vinci studio, the espresso studio, the maker lab, and the Jamie Oliver studio.

with those of classrooms to allow for both types of instruction and application to happen in the same space.[8] While I agree with the thinking behind this argument, I disagree with this approach. Putting two dysfunctional spaces together will not result in the creation of one functional space. We have already seen that traditional classrooms are poor environments for learning and that science labs also tend to be one-dimensional, because they lack the richness of learning opportunities available in a learning building.

What we need, then, is a laboratory-type space for group collaboration and hands-on project work even when the space is not being used for lab-based experiments that require access to gas, water, and electric power. For instance, you could put all the services along the perimeter or in a ceiling-hung arrangement and equip the middle of the room with a variety of movable furnishings. Other types of furnishings should also be available to permit some of the other modalities of learning, as should the opportunity to plug in mobile computing devices. Getting back to the four primordial metaphors, a well-designed science lab should support learning from a mentor (campfire), learning from peers (watering hole), learning by doing (life), as well as reflective learning (cave). That means the lab should be furnished so that students can watch a teacher-led demonstration, work collaboratively with their peers, do hands-on projects or experiments, or do independent study or research. The sidebar "Do Now: Making Labs Cost-Effective" offers suggestions for how to implement some of these changes without breaking the school bank.

The parallels between the desired learning outcomes of science education and those of other disciplines are rarely realized in the design of traditional schools. For example, scientific research methods and other processes are just as applicable in social studies and the humanities as they are in science. That is why it is important to take a more multidisciplinary approach to the design and planning of the environments where these skills will be developed. Further on in this chapter, we will look at solutions for creating cross-disciplinary learning environments where modes of learning traditionally associated only with science education are equally available to the other subject areas as well.

COMPUTER LABS

The term *computer lab* is a bit of an oxymoron. Computers provide the means to free students from the drudgery of the classroom, but a computer lab is actually nothing more than a traditional classroom with computers in it. Such an arrangement takes the most powerful agent of transformation and student empowerment that a school could possibly have (i.e., computers) and utilizes them as a surrogate for a bad teacher. Who could argue that a computer lab is welcoming and versatile, supports multiple learning modes, or sends a positive message? In fact, computers labs fail badly against all these measures. Yet they continue to exist in schools despite the strong reasons for getting rid of them.

Computer labs were instituted when the conventional wisdom was to "teach computers" as if it were just another subject. Labs were also efficient purely from a technician's point of view in that all the computers were in one place and it was

Before and After: Computer Lab

FIGURE 4.5 *Before:* A computer lab in use at the Hillel Academy of Tampa, Florida, until it underwent a low-budget renovation. During renovation, the lab was eliminated in favor of a students' common space more conducive to the use of mobile technologies.

FIGURE 4.6 *After:* The same space that used to be the computer lab at the left. It has now been transformed into a student-centered space, which is ideal for mobile computing but also for a host of other modes of learning.

easy to secure and maintain them. However, there is little pedagogical benefit to this set-up, and it is imperative to consider other ways to integrate information and communications technology in schools that prioritizes educational benefits over ease of maintenance.[9] With centralized computer labs, students have to leave their primary learning space to get structured computer instruction. As a result, computer instruction is limited to the scheduling and availability of the lab and is not necessarily connected with the ongoing curriculum.[10]

With the advent of more and more powerful mobile computing devices, educators have been moving steadily away from teaching "computers" in a computer lab. There are other good reasons for this shift. First, students are able to learn how to use computers very easily, even at a very young age. They pick up the digital cues from computer programs faster than most adults can, and children can quickly learn and even master complex programs on their own or with minimal instruction. Second, if you look at how students learn and use computers naturally, it is almost always toward achieving some specific goal rather than the mastery of the computer itself. Third, computers democratize learning by ensuring that students can acquire essential skills without necessarily learning exactly the same things at the same pace as their classmates. None of these observations would lead to the development of a lab full of computers where all students learn the same thing at the same time.

FIVE IDEAS FOR ALTERNATIVE SPACES

The following section will introduce five alternative spaces that schools will benefit from creating: the Da Vinci studio, the espresso studio, the maker lab, the Jamie Oliver studio, and the black-box theater. Each alternative space supports the six educational strategies and the four design principles referenced throughout this book.

While the transformation of one or more classrooms into Learning Studios or Suites can be relatively inexpensive, the creation of interdisciplinary labs like those described above will require more significant expenditures. Still, the cost might not be greater than the sums many schools and districts spend on renovations that do little to improve learning.

Da Vinci Studio

The Da Vinci studio is a metaphor for the twenty-first century, where the hard lines that had separated the arts and the sciences in the twentieth century are being

FIGURE 4.7   A Da Vinci studio in operation. Notice how this space at the Mid-Pacific Institute in Hawaii is set up as an interdisciplinary studio. The room has many work-stations for graphic design and computer programming and a lab area for a variety of science projects. Children are able to work with art materials, science projects, and technology. The floors are easy to clean; there is access to large work surfaces, water, and electricity; and the room connects to an outdoor deck for hands-on activities.

blurred. Instead of pigeonholing subject areas into right- or left-brain categories, schools need to make more opportunities for students to escape these restrictions and to blend different ways of thinking.[11] When my colleagues and I came up with the notion of a *Da Vinci studio*, it was to create a space that celebrated the arts as much as it did the sciences. After all, there is no better-known interdisciplinary genius than Leonardo Da Vinci. His artwork can be admired for its scientific rigor, and his scientific drawings praised for their artistic attention to detail. His workspace could be considered part artist's studio, part science lab, and part model-building shop.

The combination of curriculum, space, and resources fits well with the recommendations for the fit out of science labs and art rooms. For the design of secondary school science labs, the Association for Science Education recommends specifications for water- and chemical-resistant floors and work surfaces, adequate ventilation, natural lighting, good acoustics, vented booths, access to water and cleanup facilities, and project and prep storage.[12] These recommendations are similar to those outlined for art rooms. The studio transforms from science lab to art studio in minutes, while also allowing the area to function as both science lab and art studio simultaneously.

A well-designed Da Vinci studio would have the following qualities:

- Lots of natural lighting and ventilation
- Durable flooring that is resistant to water and easy to clean
- Ample storage—for student tools and project supplies
- Generous preparation area
- Display area for finished and in-progress work
- Access to water and cleanup facilities
- Power supplied from the floor or ceiling grid or both
- Appropriate acoustical treatments to control noise
- Transparent windows or doors to allow people from outside the studio to see in and to allow people inside the studio to see out
- Connection to an outdoor project deck through wide doors for large and messy projects

The furnishings and workspaces would be versatile enough to accommodate both 2-D (planning, drawing, and painting) and 3-D projects (model making, sculpture, craft making, and other experiments) and would allow some students to sit at a desk, others to lean on a stool at a counter-height table, and others to stand around a project bench.

Espresso Studio

Whereas the Da Vinci studio is all about hands-on work, the *espresso studio* is a place for collaboration, social interaction, and independent study. Ideally, an espresso studio would look like an espresso coffee place. However, in a school setting, one interpretation would be to design the espresso studio like a hotel lobby: a space that would allow groups or an individual to work in an informal, inviting, and relaxed fashion with easy access to snacks and beverages. Some features of the espresso studio include comfortable furnishings, high ceilings, access to the outdoors, and private zones connected to open circulation areas. Students could come and go as needed, using the space and furniture and interacting with others as they choose. The attention to detail and aesthetics needs to send to the occupants a positive message that they are of value and welcome here. Of course, schools are not hotel lobbies, but this analogy can help you understand how to plan space and furnishings that support individual work and reflection while still allowing for group work and social interaction. Designed to function like a hotel lobby, the espresso studio would be a good place to see the four design principles at work: be welcoming, be versatile, support varying and specific learning activities, and send positive messages.

FIGURE 4.8 At Magnificat High School in Cleveland, a typical cafeteria was turned into an espresso studio, which is open all day for contemplation and group work.

The Maker Lab

Around the world, the *maker* movement continues to gather steam. With the Internet as guide and the ready availability of inexpensive components, DIY enthusiasts of all ages have never had it better. According to Brit Morin, today's DIY crowd is "making gadgets like robots, printers and other programmable devices hacked together using free software and tools found across the web."[13] TechShop, a national community-based DIY chain, offers those interested in making, inventing, and tinkering access to machines and equipment like laser cutters, CNC (computer numerical control) milling machines, 3-D printers, and commercial-grade sewing machines.[14] In their book *Invent to Learn*, Sylvia Libow Martinez and Gary Stager offer a strong argument for bringing children's natural enthusiasm for making things into schools.[15] With prices continuing to drop on equipment and software, most schools can afford to set up at least a basic maker lab, where students can express their creativity by building their own inventions.

FIGURE 4.9   In this maker lab at a middle school in Washington state, a high-tech 3-D printer allows students to turn complex designs into real working models.

Martinez and Stager provide some basic criteria for a maker lab in school. They suggest a flexible space that will be suitable for multiple projects and will have lots of storage, with *flexible* defined as providing opportunities for collaboration and independent work. In my mind, the maker lab comes closest to the garage analogy I discussed at the start of this chapter. All the qualities that make a good garage workshop are also applicable to a good maker lab. While the *life* metaphor best describes the maker lab, a good design should also provide some soft seating, where students can take breaks and get into *watering hole* mode or do their own research on the Internet (*cave* mode).

Jamie Oliver Studio

There are rich, multidisciplinary learning opportunities embedded in the study of agriculture. After all, it was a chemist (Fritz Haber) who was responsible for developing the processes of now common-day fertilization, an inventor-entrepreneur (John Deere) who improved the plow that ultimately uncovered the potential in Midwestern soil, and a scientist-educator (George Washington Carver) who taught poor farmers how to develop alternative crops and developed numerous resources for the cultivation and culinary preparation of various produce. A humanitarian and agronomist (Norman Borlaug) aided a worldwide effort to reduce starvation via the development of high-yield crops.

The interdisciplinary approach of these innovative leaders offers much inspiration for a multidisciplinary studio—one that enables the study of agricultural science, chemistry, social issues, writing, innovation, entrepreneurism, and culinary arts. My colleagues and I have labeled such an area the *Jamie Oliver studio*. Although he is not a historical figure like the masters mentioned earlier, Oliver is a household name for his groundbreaking work in the area of health and nutrition—particularly in schools.

A well-designed Jamie Oliver studio would incorporate an outdoor garden space, a teaching kitchen, and a café space. The garden could be a full-fledged agricultural center or even a small plant-box herb garden, depending on space and availability. A teaching kitchen could be connected to a café with round tables and soft chairs. It would not need to be confined to four walls, but could spill over into circulation areas and perhaps onto outdoor patios. Most schools already have a commercial-grade kitchen connected to a large multipurpose space typically used as the cafeteria. With minor adjustments, this arrangement can be converted to a Jamie Oliver studio with a teaching kitchen focused on students' developing the knowledge and skills students need about proper nutrition and good health.

FIGURE 4.10 At this school in Tasmania, students run the café and kitchen areas of this Jamie Oliver studio during community events; note the outdoor connection that allows the space to expand into a large patio area.

The Jamie Oliver studio would not only be a kitchen, but would also have space and furnishings to support related instruction on nutrition, agriculture, and even food business. Ideally, the studio would be linked to a student garden where knowledge of agricultural sciences could be applied hands-on. Food that is grown and harvested in the school's garden could be used in the school's commercial kitchen to prepare healthy and nutritious meals. Excess produce could also be sold in a student-run famers market connecting the school and community while helping students develop entrepreneurial skills at the same time. Don't forget about the social and informal learning opportunities inherent in food-related experiences. A café area adjacent to the teaching kitchen could support social interaction and the development of key communication and relationship-building skills.

The Jamie Oliver studio supports three of the four primordial learning metaphors:

- *Life:* practical experience with food growth and preparation. At the very least, include small garden boxes to grow herbs and vegetables on a small scale if space is limited.
- *Campfire:* space for direct instruction of relevant subjects. Teachers can circulate and work with students in project work areas, and there is no need to create a classroom-type space.
- *Watering hole:* The café space is the place for rich, informal, and social learning experiences.

Black-Box Theater

A black-box theater, also called an experimental theater, is used in drama, music, and other performance arts to house small plays, recitals, training, and practices. The black-box theater is popular because it offers a flexible space for experimenting with sets and uses. These adaptable spaces have been built in old warehouses, abandoned restaurants, stores, cafés, nightclubs, repurposed offices, and even houses. Additionally, they are fitted with furniture that can be moved around, and layouts can be shifted and adapted to whatever the artist needs. An orchestra, a debate panel, and a ballet can all happen in the same space, with little time and cost to change between uses. In a black-box theater, users are not afraid to change things around—an attitude that contributes further to making the space a dynamic environment for learning. Because of its natural agility, the black-box theater is an almost perfect representation of the learning building.

FIGURE 4.11 This black-box theater at the American School of Bombay has vastly improved the school's music and performing arts program. The highly versatile space offers a much wider array of activities than a traditional school auditorium does.

Basically, a black-box theater includes a large, open floor with an array of special lighting and acoustic fittings within a flexible ceiling grid. A sprung wood floor is optimal because it has better acoustic qualities than other floors, is more comfortable for physical activities like dance and performance, and is more aesthetically pleasing. Foldaway bleachers can be added for viewing audiences. The advantage of this design is that the whole space of the theater is available for performance-related activities, whereas in a traditional auditorium, the audience seating area takes up the majority of the space. For schools with relatively generous renovation budgets, the conversion of its auditorium into a black-box theater is a viable option. It would entail the removal of the seats and the installation of new flooring and a lighting and acoustic grid at the ceiling. In a more sophisticated arrangement (see the photo of the American School of Bombay's well-designed black-box theater) a control booth could also be built. In the long run, a black-box theater represents an excellent investment because it returns a significant amount of underutilized space to teaching and learning. Beyond that, students will be able to benefit from professional-quality performance and music-related activities not offered within most school auditoriums.

With all the special learning areas just discussed, the idea is to provide schools with a richer palette of teaching and learning opportunities. Since the availability of these spaces will reduce the need for traditional classrooms, the incorporation of special learning areas will not necessarily increase the amount of gross floor area needed at any particular school.

Naturally, the labs discussed here are meant to be incorporated into the school's curriculum, pedagogy, and schedule. Spaces like these will enable schools to enrich their curriculum to include or enhance subjects and activities like industrial design and set design, graphic arts, professional theatrical productions, broadcasting, and health and nutrition programs. The spaces also provide opportunities to develop students' soft skills in team building, problem solving, and social-emotional development. As with all changes in design, the creation of these labs entails and allows changes in pedagogy that can be enhanced by staff-wide professional development. We refer to this form of professional development as *educational commissioning*, which represents the special training that teachers will receive before school opening to help them understand the full potential of twenty-first-century space design and the changes in curriculum, pedagogy, and scheduling that will allow educators to realize these benefits.

For the most part, the labs discussed in this chapter can be used by students of most grade levels and in most subject areas as well. How exactly the areas will be used at any given time during the day is limited only by the imagination of the teacher.

One of the biggest complaints about school is that students enjoy few opportunities to apply in a hands-on way the theoretical knowledge gained from textbooks. This chapter has shown how schools can go beyond traditional science labs to provide many varied and interesting spaces that students can use to apply their creative skills to make their educational experience more exciting and rewarding.

CHAPTER FIVE

Making Room for Collaboration

Professional Space for Teachers

ALL TOO RARELY, the environments in which teachers work support teachers working together. As we've seen, classrooms and hallways are arranged so that teachers across K–12 grades work in separate classrooms. In some cases, teachers set up their own classrooms, with their own desks in them, and claim ownership over that space. Another commonly used method for allocating space to classes in high schools is to have both teachers and students change classrooms every period. This is even worse than simply having students move from room to room, since it means that no one feels a sense of custodianship toward the space.

But while the design of school buildings tends to isolate teachers in classrooms, the field of education itself has been moving steadily toward a model that encourages greater collaboration between teachers.[1] Indeed there is evidence that reform efforts focused on improving the capabilities of individual teachers are less effective than those that engage teachers collectively.[2] This chapter will discuss the importance of teacher collaboration and how spaces can be designed to support it. As you'll see, the discussion touches on all six educational strategies, worth repeating here: student-centered learning; teacher collaboration; positive school climate; technology integration; flexible scheduling; and connection to the environment, community, and global network. The most important of these, of course, is teacher collaboration.

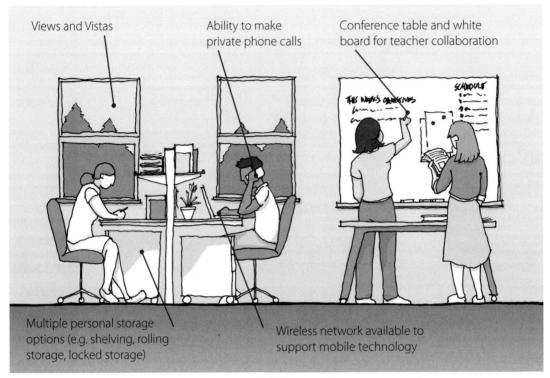

Views and Vistas

Ability to make private phone calls

Conference table and white board for teacher collaboration

Multiple personal storage options (e.g. shelving, rolling storage, locked storage)

Wireless network available to support mobile technology

FIGURE 5.1 Some Important Features of a Teacher Collaboration Space

To better facilitate teacher collaboration, teachers who work with the same group of students need to have their own workspaces near one another. This proximity facilitates common planning and informal conversations—whether the talk is about teaching strategies, curriculum materials, or the needs of particular students on any given day. Consider how many good ideas fall by the wayside in the busyness of school life when teachers work in isolation. Consider also the lost opportunities to share strategies for connecting with a struggling student when teachers are simply in different rooms.

There's no need for *all* the school's teachers to have their desks together. In fact, an all-teacher grouping will probably work against collaboration, because the whole group of teachers is likely to be too big to get initiatives off the ground. So, how do we design spaces for effective collaboration?

EFFECTIVE GROUPINGS FOR COLLABORATION

One learning-centered approach to teacher workspace is to set up teacher offices so that the staff who work with the same group of students also work on their own planning and assessment in the same space. The group might consist of generalist or specialist teachers across a grade level, or a multiage learning community. Either way, the grouping allows each student's teachers to work together.

This arrangement also gives teachers the opportunity to plan interdisciplinary projects, to capitalize on each other's knowledge and strengths, to discuss a student's progress, and to share strategies for dealing with specific learning and well-being needs. It also plays a role in allowing flexible scheduling, as teachers are able to communicate easily with each other to make changes to the (local) timetable where necessary. As a result, learning opportunities can be more easily tailored to the individual needs of students.

FIGURE 5.2 Teacher office at P. K. Yonge Developmental Research School at the University of Florida in Gainesville. Professionalism is highly regarded in this school, as it has a university connection; most of the teachers at P. K. Yonge have advanced degrees.

FIGURE 5.3 Transparent elements like glass doors or parts of walls allow teachers to meet with each other and still monitor the learning community around them.

A more common approach, especially in high schools, is to group teachers by department. Here, teachers work together across grade levels but are not necessarily working with the same students at the same time. Here, again, there is a definite bene-fit to having teachers work in a collaborative group rather than be isolated in their own specialized classrooms—the math teacher in a math classroom and a science teacher in a science classroom and so on. However, the downside with departmental groupings is that it reinforces the siloed model of education, where subjects are taught in isola-tion. This kind of grouping works against the move toward more hands-on, inter-disciplinary courses that schools across the country are attempting to implement.

Ideally, the teachers' group office will be located near their students' learning areas. In this way, the students will take most of their classes near their teachers' office. Some offices can be configured with a window overlooking nearby learning areas, so that teachers can keep an eye on students.

Teachers need to have a space in which to sit, reflect, and plan, individually and in a team. They also need a space to store their professional library and secure their belongings. This space is commonly a desk but might not always be—the same activities could also be accommodated by a room with bookshelves, filing cabinets, a large central table, an ergonomic chair for each regular office user (plus a spare), a sofa, personal lockable storage units, and laptop charging points. The "desk-free" arrangement might even be superior, as it prioritizes teachers' collaborative work, gives each individual a variety of places in which to sit and work, and gives each person more space to spread multiple books, papers, and computers on the big table. Because the table surface is shared real estate, it is also unlikely to encourage excess accumulation of disorganized personal papers in the way that personal desks often do (see the sidebar "Shifting the Center").

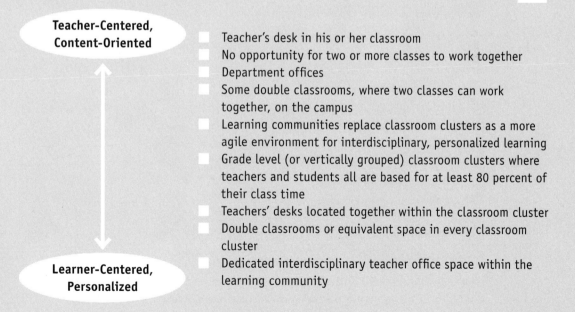

SHIFTING THE CENTER

This chart gives a brief overview of how a school's facilities can progress from being teacher-centric to learner-centric.

Teacher-Centered, Content-Oriented

- Teacher's desk in his or her classroom
- No opportunity for two or more classes to work together
- Department offices
- Some double classrooms, where two classes can work together, on the campus
- Learning communities replace classroom clusters as a more agile environment for interdisciplinary, personalized learning
- Grade level (or vertically grouped) classroom clusters where teachers and students all are based for at least 80 percent of their class time
- Teachers' desks located together within the classroom cluster
- Double classrooms or equivalent space in every classroom cluster
- Dedicated interdisciplinary teacher office space within the learning community

Learner-Centered, Personalized

Whether it comprises desks or a large central table, the design of the office should adhere to high-quality environmental standards. That is, it needs to have all of the qualities that keep our human senses switched on but not offended, like:

- Windows to the outdoors, or at the very least, to a room through which the outdoors can be seen
- Storage options such as shelving and rolling and fixed storage units
- Wireless network to support the use of laptops, tablets, and smartphones
- Conference table large enough to accommodate all the teachers working within a particular learning community
- Fixed or movable whiteboard or other writing, display, and presentation surface
- Fit-for-purpose artificial lighting: pendants with a high color-rendition index, augmented with desk and reading lamps
- Good air quality, with natural ventilation if possible
- A pleasant atmosphere that is not excessively noisy

FIGURE 5.4 This teachers' office at Hillel Academy of Tampa, Florida, used to be a classroom. It is now part of a learning community where teachers work as a team.

FIGURE 5.5 Another view of the teachers' office at Hillel Academy. This space not only encourages collaboration among teachers, but also reduces the sense of ownership of one classroom, an important step in creating a student-centered curriculum.

Teachers are sometimes concerned that they need space away from their students in "noncontact time," which leads them to question the idea of the learning-community-based teacher office. However, the concern can be fairly easily managed. A sign on the office door could let students know who is on duty and who is not, with the community understanding that off-duty teachers should only be contacted via email. I also often hear teachers complain that they need an acoustically secure space for occasional private phone calls or meetings with students or parents, away from their colleagues. This reasonable request can be dealt within the context of a learning-community-based office, by having a small, acoustically secure room available for both students and teachers. The room would probably mainly be used by students who are working on something particularly noisy or particularly quiet, at odds with the noise level of the wider community space.

NECESSARY OR NOT? THE TEACHERS' LOUNGE

A teachers' lounge is a nice thing to have, but it is really important to ask about the purpose of a lounge if it is in your school. If there are no alternative places for teachers to meet with each other during the school day, a staff room may be necessary for that purpose. If, however, teachers have dedicated office space, a teachers' lounge probably isn't necessary.

Teachers may want a place to socialize during lunch breaks. But do teachers need a separate room to eat lunch in, or could they just as easily share café or cafeteria space with students? In many schools, the teachers do share the space, and the arrangement has a great impact on creating a positive school climate. Rather than setting up an us-and-them dichotomy of space, mirrored by the need for a teacher to be "on duty," "policing" student behavior, the sharing of dining space by teachers and students often creates a sense of family-like communion. As part of this, teachers can model the kind of behavior that makes for peaceful, sociable, and friendly mealtimes.

Other functions of the teachers' lounge can also be provided for in different settings around the school. In fact, the more flexible the school design, the more opportunities there are for teachers to take advantage of other spaces. Collaborative planning and assessment can happen in teachers' professional offices. Whole-of-staff meetings must happen out of school hours, anyway, so teachers then have the ability to use any large commons or meeting space. Likewise, special social celebrations can happen in any indoor space not being used at recess or lunchtime, such

DO NOW: A LOW-COST FOCAL SPACE FOR TEACHERS

Without renovating, you can still support teachers with collaborative workspace. Think creatively about how to eke out grade-level offices for groups of two to five teachers. Even if teachers still spend most of their time in their classrooms, they are able to have a professional workspace for activities like collaborative planning and assessment, which do not involve contact with students.

One idea involves converting part of a larger classroom into a teachers' office by simply installing a table for collaborative work, a bookshelf for teachers' professional libraries, a filing cabinet for current planning and assessment papers, and some small lockable storage units for teachers' belongings. The table might be used by students during class time, but would give a focal point for the local teaching team during their out-of-hours planning and assessment time.

as a learning studio or multipurpose common area. See the sidebar "Do Now: A Low-Cost Focal Space for Teachers" for other ideas on how to create a collaborative space for teachers.

At Preshil, The Margaret Lyttle Memorial School, a small elementary school in Melbourne, Australia, ten teachers have taken to sharing their lunch around a table in one of the classrooms. All of the classrooms have a kitchenette so there are facilities to heat up food and to brew coffee and tea. Students are free to come and visit the adults at break times, either for first aid or just for a chat. The resulting atmosphere is very relaxed and friendly and contributes to the school's reputation as a place where every member of the community is valued.

There are many North American schools without teachers' lounges, but most schools haven't the alternative of teachers' offices, cafés, or learning communities and instead face the clique-fostering situation of each teacher owning his or her own classroom. While the initial intent at University Park Campus School in Worcester, Massachusetts, was to build a lounge when funding permitted, once the school was operating without it, there didn't seem to be a strong need for a lounge. In fact, its absence was viewed as having positive outcomes. Here, the intimate size of the school requires teachers to do their planning and assessment work in the school's classrooms, none of which is owned by any one teacher. Teachers eat lunch with students, and the positive school climate here is notable. I don't advocate removing or disallowing dedicated teacher workspace by any means. However, the story at University Park Campus School shows that teacher collaboration and a positive school climate can be fostered, even unintentionally, through design in unlikely ways.

The bottom line of space redesign for teachers is to empower them to do the best job they can, which is more likely to happen if they are placed within the context of a caring community of their peers.

CHAPTER SIX

Putting People and Ideas Together

The Changing Role of the School Library

GOOD LIBRARIES HAVE always been places where personalized learning happens. Libraries are less about teaching and more about learning. They are places for individual and group research, where the users are invited to ask their big and little questions, to explore their daily whims and lifelong passions, and to do so at their own pace. Libraries are actually a great template for the design of entire schools. Yet in the digital age, their role is questioned—if Google can help us access all of the information we need, and books are increasingly found on mobile devices rather than on the shelf, why do we need libraries?

This chapter examines the changing role of the school library and appropriate design responses. When it comes to deciding where the library fits into the scheme of a twenty-first-century design, the schools we have worked with fall into three categories. Some schools choose to keep and upgrade their existing library, some choose to close their central library and decentralize their collection, and some choose to change the library so that it becomes part of a larger activity center. There is also a trend toward smaller overall collections. However, even when the library's

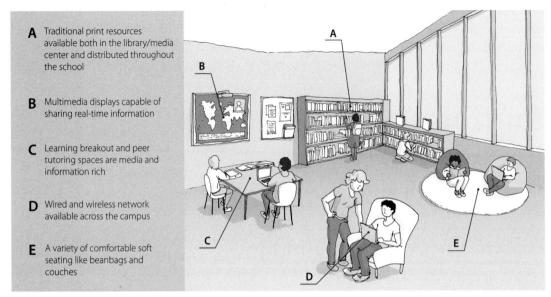

A   Traditional print resources available both in the library/media center and distributed throughout the school

B   Multimedia displays capable of sharing real-time information

C   Learning breakout and peer tutoring spaces are media and information rich

D   Wired and wireless network available across the campus

E   A variety of comfortable soft seating like beanbags and couches

FIGURE 6.1   Some Features of a Good School Library

resources are decentralized, schools continue to keep a curated collection that can be searched so that any particular volume can be retrieved fairly easily. Regardless of the course that any particular school might take, I believe firmly that from a design perspective, the essential qualities of libraries make them a source of joy for students of all ages and that schools should make every effort to preserve those qualities.[1]

WHAT IS A LIBRARY FOR?

At its heart, a library is not about storing books. If libraries were only about storing books, the space wouldn't have doors or shelves; we would just put the books in a big box and seal it up. Libraries are about connecting people with ideas. So we need to ask ourselves, "Where are the ideas?" and "Where are the people?" (see the sidebar "Information Access Before and After the Internet").

Before the advent of the Internet, all of the knowledge of humanity was either stored in people's brains or recorded on a physical medium—a book, magazine,

INFORMATION ACCESS BEFORE AND AFTER THE INTERNET

	Where Are the People?	Where Are the Recorded Ideas or Texts?
Pre-Internet era	Looking for things to read in person at the library	At the library, bookshop, newsdealer, or record store
Internet era	Using their computers and handheld digital devices to access the Internet; physically freed from the need to be at the library	Online—available for free or to be purchased by individuals or libraries; library copies accessed with member-only intranet services

journal, film, CD, DVD, cassette, vinyl record, microfiche, and so forth. In those days, libraries made perfect sense as a location for connecting people with ideas—a physical location was very important for housing the physical media in cataloged order so that people could find the information they were looking for.

The last twenty years have witnessed a massive revolution in information creation, storage, and access, as more and more of our information and communication happens via the Internet. The physical epicenter of this change is the library. I am not saying that the Internet has destroyed or will destroy the library. But the library needs a massive change to stay true to its goal of connecting people with ideas.

TEACHER-LIBRARIANS

Educators have seen that Internet search engines can put people and ideas together, but for many reasons, simple searches can result in a poor collection of texts. Some of this failure is on the part of Google—its algorithms have been exploited by page builders to generate maximum traffic for their sites without the sites' actually having the best information out there. Also, just going online and googling something does not give students the power of searching their school's intranet and the purchased electronic resources available on it. However, the biggest barrier to effective information search is actually not the search tools but the user. For so many reasons, students need help with finding what they want, whether that's because they are inexperienced at searching and don't know how to exclude certain types of sites from their results, or because they are not able to differentiate between good and bad information.

Educators understand that a search engine is not a teacher. They know Google can't develop an inquiry-based learning project that takes the best resources of the physical and virtual worlds and leads students on a personalized learning journey. This sort of complex combination of guidance, knowledge, and creativity requires a specially trained educator. In this capacity, a teacher-librarian is ideally positioned to work with teachers and students to help both groups access and evaluate all of the most relevant resources. This specifically trained educator is also uniquely suited to collaborate with other teachers to develop units of work using those resources. The teacher-librarian's role was summarized very well by North Carolina teacher-librarian and blogger Jennifer LaGarde:

> The future librarian is an instructional leader and partner who works with teachers and administrators to build school-wide collections that are accessible beyond the walls of the library and that defy traditional delivery methods. She builds a library presence centered around both physical and digital spaces for conversation, creativity and collaboration. She and her students blog, Tweet, and share their work in collaborative online spaces. The future librarian embraces social media and uses it to build a bridge between students, teachers and the world. She understands that in order to meet student needs, the library must be accessible anytime, anywhere.[2]

LaGarde goes on to say that the future is now and that effective school librarians are doing these things now.

Libraries are also good places for after-hour community meetings and small presentations. These hidden benefits of libraries are now becoming more evident as schools realize that libraries are not simply places to store books.

A VIRTUAL LIBRARY?

A well-designed school will allow students access to the school's e-book, music, and film collections whenever and wherever they wish, because after all, libraries are in the business of connecting people with ideas. This can be done by allowing students to access these resources from laptops, tablets, and even smartphones no matter where in the school the students are physically located.

Social media also brings a new dimension to libraries. Collaboration and communication can happen remotely, and a librarian can assist students and teachers without needing to be in the same place they are. Many school librarians spend more time assisting students via instant-messaging services than they do assisting students in the same room, with the benefit of an instant record of the conversation

FIGURE 6.2 Libraries are no longer the only places where students can find needed information, but even traditionally equipped libraries can offer places to read, collaborate, and do research—the kind of relaxing, comfortable places that are hard to find anywhere else in school.

being made, and online references shared with a simple "Ctrl+V." As you can see, a smaller library does not mean a smaller role for librarians.

Does this mean there would be no point in having a physical library? No. Paper books—still being published, read aloud by parents to their children, and curled up with under the shade of a tree or the warm light streaming through a window—are still very much alive. However, the more time people spend with electronic media, the less time they have available for printed media. So print collections seem set to become smaller but not to disappear altogether. That said, students can still enjoy an e-book on a Kindle or a Nook or an iPad, relaxing in the same manner as if they were reading a paper book. In other words, the lack of printed media does not automatically mean that we should also lose the enduring qualities that make libraries a relaxing and enjoyable place. The reduction in print materials will free up space in traditional libraries and can be used for student exhibitions and community meetings. Fewer books also means more space to store electronic media and equipment like laptops, tablets, and video cameras that students can borrow. Library spaces could also be used for high-end laser cutters and 3-D printers that students can access within the library and remotely from other parts of the school.

LIBRARIES ACROSS THE CAMPUS

Rather than a shrinking print library confined to an ever more sparsely used space, there should be plenty of reading places spread throughout the campus. Such places should have comfortable seating like sofas and beanbags and should be bathed in natural light, or artificial light augmented with reading lamps.

Resources also need to be available all over the school, and with the combination of digital catalogs and e-books, there is no problem administering this. Print resources are more difficult to disperse successfully, but schools are now finding effective ways to do so. One option is to have within learning communities satellite libraries whose books can be checked out by students using digital scanners.

Satellite libraries may also mean the elimination of the central school library altogether. This is the approach being used at the American School of Bombay. The school's elementary campus is housed in a six-story tower, which was originally designed for commercial offices. Personalized, independent learning is a cornerstone concept of the school, as is allowing students continual, independent access to learning resources. Each floor has its own media resource center (MRC), which teachers can supervise from the adjacent glass-walled learning studios. A librarian

FIGURE 6.3 Floor pillows for younger students make reading more comfortable and the space more home-like.

(with the skills to help students and teachers connect with appropriate printed and digital resources) is based in each MRC. Teachers felt they would be able to maximize student library access if the MRC were shared with a smaller number of classes and located just outside the learning-studio door.

The MRCs provide resources for all ages in the school and the surrounding community. One zone of each MRC is set up for students undertaking one-to-one tutoring. Parents, too, are embraced as important users of the MRCs. Each MRC therefore includes a small collection for parents, since many books of interest to expatriates are not easily accessible in Mumbai. Moreover, the furnishings of the resource centers encourage parents to read with their children there at pickup and drop-off times.

Learning-community-based schools can successfully house print collections in their principal learning spaces, since their "classroom libraries" are instantly accessible by between 50 and 125 students, as well as easily by the "visiting" students

FIGURE 6.4 A typical MRC (Media Resource Center) located within each small Learning Community at the American School of Bombay.

from other learning communities, not just the 25 who could access the libraries in a traditional classroom.

The rationale for distributing resources across the campus is strong. Just as laptops and tablets on charging trolleys are preferable to computer labs (the trolleys allow students and teachers access to computers as needed and thus facilitate personalized learning), the replication of library functions around the campus also enables more-personalized learning. In a regular classroom setting, a teacher would normally have to book a space in the library for students to do research, whether or not all students actually needed to do research in that period. With many of the library resources available in the principal learning area (classroom, learning studio, or learning community), the students have the freedom to use the things they need without taking up a whole class's allocation.

The combination of these factors means that libraries will become much smaller physically or will sometimes be eliminated altogether. This reduction or elimination of the physical library space is acceptable only if students and teachers are still able to connect with ideas (i.e., don't fire your teacher-librarian!) and if the physical environment throughout the school is library-like.

WHAT CAN YOU DO WITH AN UNDERUSED LIBRARY?

If your school has adopted many of these strategies to ensure that students are getting continual access to the best resources (not just the free Internet) in their principal learning spaces, you may find yourself with a large, underutilized space that used to be the library. What to do with that space? Trying to keep it as a central library is fine, but perhaps it could take on other roles as well, as the print collection shrinks. For instance, it could include a café, a hands-on creative space, or an audio-visual recording studio so that the space remains a lovely, big invitation to creativity and discovery (see the sidebar "Bookless School Libraries?").

FIGURE 6.5　At Magnificat High School in Cleveland, an old library was renovated to include a variety of furniture and Wi-Fi to create an area that acts more like a commons.

BOOKLESS SCHOOL LIBRARIES?

Bookless libraries are already here. BiblioTech is a completely digital library in San Antonio, Texas. Located in an underserved, largely Hispanic community, this bookless library is already a success. In the fall of 2013, the library opened with a collection of ten thousand e-books, audio books, and software training databases that members can access remotely. However, BiblioTech has not done away with the idea of the library as a place to visit, says Laura Cole, BiblioTech's special projects coordinator: "Our digital library is stored in the cloud, so you don't have to come in to get a book. But we're a traditional library in that the building itself is an important community space."*

In this book, I have not recommended bookless school libraries, but here are some elements of the BiblioTech model that schools can start to adopt immediately:

- Provide basic e-book readers to students who don't have one.
- Allow students to electronically check out as many books as possible—even those that may be available in the school's print collection.
- Offer in-school high-end technology access for students and after-hours digital literacy classes to community residents.
- Serve as a relaxing, comfortable place for students to learn, do Internet research and read quietly.

*Julianne Pepitone, "The First Bookless Library: BiblioTech Offers only e-Books," *CNN Money*, October 8, 2013, http://money.cnn.com/2013/10/08/technology/innovation/bibliotech-ebook-library/index.html?iid=HP_LN.

You might find, however, that these functions are already part of the school's learning communities and so those invitations to creativity and discovery exist in the students' principal learning spaces. In that case, maybe the library could be transformed into a home base for two to four teachers and their allocated students, as one learning community. If your school hasn't got any team teaching space, the library might be a good place to allow teachers to start practicing their full-time collaboration.

Public School 106 in Brooklyn transformed an underused attic space into a light-filled library that celebrates inquiry. The new space isn't unique in the sense of its relationship to the whole school, but it is a good example of the library as a beautiful and inspiring space in an otherwise limited, traditional school building. The transformed attic is one of few spaces in the school where two classes can work together and where students are encouraged by design to pursue their own research interests and to embark on learning independently and in small groups. The mezzanine level and the steps leading up to it provide an element of variety and excitement in the space. Speech-bubble graphics on the curved walls prompt further questions from students.[3]

COMMUNITY LIBRARIES

Community libraries can also be a great asset for schools. Becoming acquainted with the physical and electronic resources available at the local library and how to access them is a skill that will remain relevant and habitual to students after their formal schooling has finished. Moreover, the broader borrower base and multiple funding sources means that the library can purchase more resources. If your local community library is right next door, you could consider merging the two libraries. If the library is further afield, investigate ways for your students to access the library's e-book collection.

While cooperative arrangements make sense, logistically they are not simple, because schools and libraries are almost always under different jurisdictional authorities with separate lines of funding. A shared library may also raise issues of security when students—particularly very young children—and adult members of the community occupy the library at the same time. Nevertheless, the benefits of sharing are often worth the extra time and effort to work through the logistical and operational issues associated with this approach.

At Mawson Lakes School, an elementary school in Adelaide, Australia, the local library doubles as a library for the school. This was an intentional design from the time of the center's founding in 2005, and it is financed jointly by the department of education and the local government.

The joint facility has been extremely successful in offering students access to a very broad range of resources, but the down side of the arrangement is that students have limited freedom to access the library's resources any time. To combat this limitation, the school has also established reading areas around the school and

FIGURE 6.6 At Mawson Lakes School in Australia, the local public library serves as the school's library.

a reading nook with books that can be accessed at any time by the students. The combination works well to ensure that students have fast access to electronic and print texts when they are working independently as well as access to a broad range of materials during scheduled library visits.

Cooperative arrangements have worked well for older students, too. Many senior high schools are also colocated with universities and students have use of the university library.

THE FUTURE OF SCHOOL LIBRARIES

There is no point maintaining a space that's no longer relevant. Work out what is sacred about a library—a professional teacher-librarian, accessible resources, ample quiet reading space—and make sure every such element is available to students and

DO NOW: TURNING OVER A NEW LEAF IN THE SCHOOL LIBRARY

Depending on the resources available to you, you might make some of the following changes to your standard library. The lists starts with the easiest and ends with the most difficult changes:

1. Where room sizes permit and where teachers are enthusiastic, encourage the decentralization of library resources by bringing books into classrooms. Classroom-based minilibraries can be developed at minimal cost and often at no cost at all with donations from parents and local businesses.

2. Develop casual reading spaces in the library so that they are inviting and comfortable. Sofas are essential in every library. A teacher who had renovated her learning spaces began with a secondhand sofa while awaiting the construction of her new furniture, which included child-sized soft seating, but no sofa. Until it was gone, she didn't realize that the sofa was irreplaceable, as it was a magnet for elementary kids to sit and read with their parents. Beanbags are inexpensive and cozy, and you can invest in a decent number without their taking up too much space. Invest!

3. Call for two teachers to volunteer to use the library instead of their classrooms to team-teach in, during a school term. This is particularly useful if you don't have a double classroom available.

4. Distribute library resources throughout the school—particularly in commons areas so that reading can happen anytime, anywhere.

5. Redesign your library interior to incorporate a multimedia recording studio. Many traditional libraries have associated computer labs. With the increasing power of Internet-connected wireless laptops and tablets, these labs are quickly becoming obsolete. A good way to utilize this space is to get rid of the old desktop PCs and redesign the room so that it becomes a media production and recording studio. One wall can be painted green and serve as the green screen for productions. Depending on how much money is available, schools can also consider adding a live broadcast studio in the space so that the school can have its own internal radio or TV station.

teachers anytime, anywhere. To accomplish this goal, you might need a library, but be open to the idea that other spaces might do the job better in your school. The sidebar "Do Now: Turning Over a New Leaf in the School Library" summarizes some of these ideas.

School libraries have run self-administered borrowing programs for many years. Older elementary students, middle school students, and high school students are perfectly capable of checking out books on their own. There doesn't need to be a radio-frequency identification (RFID) system on every door to every room containing books. Sure, some volumes might go missing, but the expense of setting up large-scale security systems is probably greater than small losses of books every year.

For the time being at least, printed material will coexist with electronic media. However, there is a steady move away from print media in favor of the convenience of carrying, in a backpack, dozens if not hundreds of books stored on an electronic device. So, although libraries must be redesigned to allow for the ongoing migration of information to electronic media, they can continue to serve as comfortable places.

Finally, with the steeply falling prices of production equipment, schools have an opportunity to do something different with the spaces that traditional libraries once occupied. No longer are libraries just places for the passive consumption of content. In reconfigured libraries, students can actively create print and electronic media, from magazines and books to documentaries and short films and even apps and other software.

CHAPTER SEVEN

Beyond the Classroom Window

Bringing Learning Outdoors

SINCE THIS CHAPTER is about outdoor learning, urban schools and schools on small sites may assume that this discussion does not apply to them. In fact, that is far from the truth. Students who live in urban settings have an even greater need to connect with outdoors and natural settings, since these young people are most likely to suffer from "nature-deficit disorder." In an influential *New York Times* opinion piece, Timothy Egan credits Richard Louv with coining this term and cites Louv's 2005 book, *Last Child in the Woods*, which says that "kids who do play outside are less likely to get sick, to be stressed or become aggressive, and are more adaptable to life's unpredictable turns."[1] The discussion, the recommendations, and even many of the specific examples of outdoor learning areas in this chapter apply to urban settings as much as they do to rural settings.

THE IMPORTANCE OF NATURE FOR HUMAN DEVELOPMENT

My recommendation that learning spaces should be connected visually and physically to nature is supported by Rachel Kaplan and Stephen Kaplan's attention

FIGURE 7.1 Imaginative use of outdoor areas: children playing the drums in an outdoor plaza at Learning Gate Community School in Lutz, Florida.

restoration theory. As described in chapter 1, this theory provides a framework for identifying environments with "soft fascinations" that are beneficial for cognitive restoration and performance. Soft fascinations are scenes or objects that one can observe with effortless attention, for example, leaves rustling in the wind, water running over pebbles in a creek, or clouds slowly moving in the sky.[2]

Several studies have identified that connections to nature help relieve cognitive fatigue and improve a person's ability to concentrate. Similar studies have shown that interactions with nature are beneficial for children with symptoms of attention deficit/hyperactivity disorder (ADHD). An individual's perceived level of safety and opportunities to be in environments that foster meditation and personal reflection have also been identified as having restorative benefits.

A *New York Times* piece, by Tara Parke-Pope, quotes Andrea Faber Taylor, a child environment and behavior researcher at the Landscape and Human Health Laboratory at the University of Illinois at Urbana–Champaign, who said, "We advocate that children be given views of green space from the classroom. We've done research on children in public housing that shows the ones who have a green view perform better."[3]

Walk past any school during class time, and you are often struck by how quiet it is, for a place full of children or young adults. Not only are the students not heard, but they're rarely seen at that time, either. Maybe one class is out in the yard playing an organized game, or a physical education teacher is working with a class somewhere outside on the campus. Apart from that, it's devoid of life. Academic work takes place indoors 99 percent of the time. Why is this? It doesn't make much sense for an institution concerned primarily with enhancing children's exploration of the world to expect the exploration to happen almost exclusively within four walls. Traditional school design offers teachers few opportunities to seamlessly extend learning activities beyond the classroom. Even in those rare cases where suitable outdoor learning areas are created, there is no guarantee that teachers will utilize these areas. Outdoor learning may be perceived as inferior to indoor learning, especially if it is not clearly connected to the curriculum or—in this day and age—to what's on the test.

Nonetheless, research suggests a number of reasons why outdoor learning should be incorporated into the school day—and the school design. Recent findings indicate:

- Children with symptoms of ADHD are better able to concentrate after contact with nature.[4] ,
- Play in a diverse natural environment reduces or eliminates bullying.[5]
- Nature helps children develop powers of observation and creativity and instills a sense of peace and being at one with the world.[6]
- Early experiences with the natural world have been positively linked with the development of imagination and the sense of wonder.[7]
- Wonder is an important motivator for lifelong learning.[8]
- Children who play in nature have more positive feelings about each other.[9]
- A decrease in children's time spent outdoors is contributing to an increase in myopia in developed countries.[10]
- Outdoor environments are important to children's development of independence and autonomy.[11]

So what does all this teach us about the design of learning environments? We should consider the following:

- Connect to nature via views to the outdoors and connections to outdoor spaces like patios, gardens, and play areas. Even in dense urban settings (or perhaps more so in such settings), connections to nature are important and can be achieved by having large windows through which the sky is visible. See the sidebar "Outdoor Learning in Urban Settings."
- Where no outside greenery is visible, bring some in. Grow indoor plants by windows.
- Connections to nature also include class pets. Make room for small animals like hamsters, turtles, or rabbits, and find a place for an aquarium with interesting and colorful fish that students can take care of.
- Provide "cave" spaces for personal reflection where students can get away from the crowd.
- Ensure that informal learning areas connected to nature feel safe and are welcoming and comfortable.

NATURE AND EDUCATIONAL STRATEGIES

Consider the ways in which well-planned outdoor environments can support the following six educational strategies outlined in chapter 1.

Student-centered learning means learning that is personalized and controlled by each student, so that the children aren't all doing the same thing at the same time. An outdoor space available for learning and adjacent to the indoor learning spaces allows a broader scope and inspiration for students' short-term and long-term projects.

Technology integration can be supported in outdoor spaces. The outdoors provides rich subject matter for photography and video narrative—subject matter that is very limited in a classroom setting. With the increasing range and bandwidth offered by wireless networks, along with reduced costs, shaded outdoor areas adjacent to indoor areas offer pleasant and less distracting spots for students to work with mobile technologies like laptops, tablets, and smartphones. Outdoor learning also exposes students to technology they might not be able to use within a classroom. Outside, students can become familiar with tools such as survey instruments, water and soil testing equipment, and even some older "technologies" like sundials and weather vanes.

OUTDOOR LEARNING IN URBAN SETTINGS

Even though urban kids are more likely than suburban or rural kids to suffer from nature-deficit disorder discussed earlier in this chapter, urban schools tend to have fewer opportunities for sending students outdoors, in communion with nature. Many urban sites are so highly built up that they leave little room for green areas and restful outdoor zones. However, with a little imagination, underutilized areas can be converted at minimal expense to serve outdoor learning activities. My advice to urban schools is to think small, as in a small vegetable patch, a small fishpond, a small seating and reading area, or a small fountain. Where there is, literally, no room on the site to locate outdoor learning activities, consider using the roof of the school building for learning activities. Rooftop learning may include vegetable gardens, weather stations, and canopied areas for individual and group seating for activities such as reading, research, independent study, and team collaboration.

The small outdoor areas at Meadowdale Middle School and at Saint Martin De Porres High School, both pictured here, illustrate how outdoor learning opportunities can be created even on tighter urban sites.

FIGURE 7.2   This outdoor nature lab at Meadowdale Middle School in Lynnwood, Washington, has been given privacy from the local neighborhood through the creation of a berm with natural plantings.

FIGURE 7.3   Here at Saint Martin de Porres High School in Cleveland, an urban garden is maintained by the students for the benefit of the local community.

Through *flexible scheduling*, a student who is particularly passionate about a particular project is not always forced to interrupt his or her work because the bell has rung at the end of the forty-five-minute period. Using the outside space as well as the inside space can afford students and teachers more flexibility to continue work beyond the bell, even when another group of students is moving into the inside space.

The creative use of a permeable indoor-outdoor space can allow *teacher collaboration*. For instance, two teachers can work together in an arrangement where one teacher works indoors with a small group of students, conferencing or providing roundtable discussion, while the other teacher supervises students at work outdoors.

Functional and beautiful outdoor spaces can help to foster a *positive school climate* because they help students to relax and reflect. Robin Moore's 1996 study revealed that children who play in nature have more positive feelings about each other. So replanting and otherwise enhancing the campus's natural features can be important for social and emotional development.[12]

Obviously the sixth educational strategy, *connection to the environment*, is most strongly supported by functional outdoor learning spaces. Connecting the indoor spaces to the outdoors is just one element of the strategy. Preserving and enhancing the campus's natural features, including topography, watercourses, trees, and shrubs, is another.

OUTDOOR ENVIRONMENTS AND LEARNING MODALITIES

Of the twenty learning modalities explained in chapter 3, none cannot be supported outdoors.[13] To be fair, you might not wish to engage in certain modalities outdoors if the temperature were too cold or if it were raining, but in mild to warm, dry weather, every single modality could occur outside. And some of the modalities, such as naturalist learning, are supported far better outside than inside.

All the different kinds of learning that can happen outside will fall under one or more of these three categories:

- *Play:* Gross and fine motor coordination, creativity, and social skills are developed in outdoor play.
- *Fieldwork (study of the outside world):* Outdoors, students can physically examine the natural and human processes and designs that make up our world (and, ironically, what science, geography, and social studies textbooks are full of).

■ *Inside goes outside:* The kind of solo, paired, or group computer-based or book-based study largely happens indoors, but it can just as easily happen outdoors for much of the year in most climates.

These three categories allow us to think carefully about the different design requirements for each of these broader learning goals. The new way of thinking about learning lessens the chance that we will write off the outside environment as "too cold" or "too wet" or "too hot," because we will have thought about what kinds of learning aren't so affected by which particular climate factors.

For example, sitting still is unpleasantly cold if it is around sixty degrees Fahrenheit. Being physically active when it's that temperature is absolutely fine, however, and physical activity includes gross motor play and outdoor fieldwork.

Designing for Play

Play is an important learning modality. It is also the oldest learning modality because it's how we've evolved to learn. Play is also increasingly important because of rising rates of obesity among children.

A 2012 survey of children by the Heart Foundation of Australia found that the kinds of play features children want are not overly manicured; instead, they're a little scruffy: "Hills to roll, run, and slide down, . . . rocks and tunnels to scramble around, . . . branches and leaves with which to build tree houses and cubbies and community art. Water was essential." "They also want to be challenged by their play areas sometimes, to be a little bit frightened" according to a spokeswoman for the Heart Foundation. "They want to be able to build and construct things, so we need to provide moveable parts, debris, . . . not to blow all the twigs away with a blower but perhaps even plant trees that drop their leaves."[14] It's quite a different picture from the ubiquitous plastic-molded slippery slide and monkey bars that you'll find in most playgrounds.

Play spaces should pose open-ended questions. They should prompt imaginative responses. They should foster a connection between the players and the natural environment. If you are keen to invest in improving your school's play spaces, before jumping to choose a ready-made climbing gym from a catalog, consider how much better you could build it from scratch. There is great inspiration to be found online—several bloggers collect pictures and reviews of outstanding play spaces from around the world. Employ a professional designer if you can, but more importantly, have students participate in the design process, and have

FIGURE 7.4 *Designing for Play* An unstructured area with an assortment of natural elements inspires more creative play than a structured playground does.

your professional designer work alongside the students (see the sidebar "Successful Play Spaces").

Designing for Fieldwork

School design needs to support what the current education literature on project and experiential learning argues for: the importance of hands-on, active, lifelong learning. *Fieldwork* describes the firsthand collection of data through sensory observation in an urban, rural, or natural environment. It could be as simple as two-year-olds feeling the difference between sand, mud, and snow on their fingers, or five-year-olds counting the number of trees on the campus, or ten-year-olds filming the nesting habits of a bird. Considering that hands-on activities like these are often

SUCCESSFUL PLAY SPACES

This helpful set of ten design principles for play is suggested by the organization Play England:

Successful play spaces . . .

- are "bespoke" [tailored to fit the specific needs of school and site]
- are well located
- make use of natural elements
- provide a wide range of play experiences
- are accessible to both disabled and non-disabled children
- meet community needs
- allow children of different ages to play together
- build in opportunities to experience risk and challenge
- are sustainable and appropriately maintained
- allow for change and evolution*

*Aileen Shackell, Nicola Butler, Phil Doyle, and David Ball, for Play England, Design for Play: A Guide to Creating Successful Play Spaces (Nottingham, UK: DCSF Publications, 2008), www .playengland.org.uk/media/70684/design-for-play.pdf.

more effective than passive activities for lifelong learning, schools need to value fieldwork and design areas that support this key modality of learning.

Design for fieldwork on campus largely means maintaining and enhancing the special features of the campus's natural environment (see the sidebar "Do Now: Making the Most of Your Outdoor Space"). Watercourses are a wonderful asset for fieldwork and can be replanted to provide a habitat for native birds and other animals. Wooded areas are all too often demolished to make way for development, but they make great learning places. In fact, proponents of the German *Waldschule* (forest school) movement specifically seek out forests in which to base outdoor

FIGURE 7.5 *Designing for Fieldwork* Woods and ponds to explore and study wildlife are of more interest to students than large stretches of asphalt or grass.

classrooms. Don't be intimidated by the word *forest*. On many smaller urban sites, a small grove of trees can support its own ecosystem that is worth studying.

Even without these kinds of environments on campus, a school may be able to take advantage of adjacent and nearby public parks. Sites can be chosen for new school developments that take into account the proximity of public parks.

In the early childhood years, outdoor fieldwork looks very much like play, as toddlers and preschoolers are given time and space to freely explore and observe, using all their senses, the qualities of the natural environment. Through the elementary years, inquiry-based study of the natural environment can begin, as the children develop an understanding of the observable art and science present outdoors. School designers who understand that such activities can be a valuable piece

DO NOW: MAKING THE MOST OF YOUR OUTDOOR SPACE

Without presuming to know anything about your particular location's climate and your school's architecture, not to mention the resources available, I can offer some suggestions that will enhance your outdoor areas for different learning modalities and support the six educational strategies (student-centered learning; teacher collaboration; positive school climate; technology integration; flexible scheduling; and connection to the environment, community, and global network). Depending on the resources available to you, you might be able to do some of the following on this list, which starts with the easiest and ends with the most difficult changes:

- In some cases, you may have suitable outdoor areas that are simply not being used. As a school designer, I have found that in cases like these, schools need to actively build in outdoor learning experiences into the students' learning day. Sometimes teachers simply forget that the schoolyard is part of their palette of spaces to use. Prompt some outdoor activity using the staff-room bulletin board, social media, or internal email to highlight the learning opportunities or activities that *are* being done outside.

- Conduct or commission a study by students of the use of your school's outdoor areas. Survey students and teachers, and use observational technique to develop a picture of how much the outdoor spaces are used and for what kinds of activities, particularly what kinds of play. Find out what is holding your school community back from going outside more often. Use the results to inform your decision making.

- Begin work to make sure that the outdoor space adjacent to classrooms is usable, if there is such outdoor space. This means unlocking doors and moving existing outdoor furniture into a location where a supervising teacher can see it from the windows.

- If some of the indoor learning spaces at your school have adjacent outdoor learning spaces and they are not being well used by the classes in them, consider how these areas can be made more usable from a teaching and learning perspective. For example, a small green area could become a vegetable garden, and an unused outdoor area immediately adjacent to the school building may only need some suitable furniture to become usable.

continued

DO NOW: MAKING THE MOST OF YOUR OUTDOOR SPACE, *continued*

☐ Make simple changes to your school's outdoor play facilities to enhance the scope for different kinds of play and different ages of students. The changes can begin simply, for instance, with the provision of some materials and a dedicated space for building forts. Install permanent vertical poles that could support forts, if you don't have the luxury of a forested area on site. It might mean providing a range of different portable equipment for physical play, such as stilts.

☐ Seek out opportunities on your campus to create outdoor learning terraces. Wherever an existing garden, courtyard, or balcony sits directly outside an external classroom door, you can create an outdoor learning terrace by placing outdoor furniture there and improving glazing if necessary between the room and the outside. If there's no door, perhaps you can install one. Involve students in the design and consultation as much as you can.

☐ Add more greenery to the campus. Have students research the indigenous plants of your region, and enlist the efforts of a local arborist to restore unused areas of the school grounds to resemble this original environment. You can do this in any location, even in the middle of a big city, where its effect is most striking! The addition of greenery offers several learning benefits: the scientific and geographic study of the local area, the hands-on learning involved in actually cultivating the plants, the future benefits of an on-site resource for fieldwork, and a natural play-scape.

☐ Enhance the indoor-outdoor connections across the campus by replacing walls, windows, and small doors with large garage-style doors or bifold doors that can be left open when the weather cooperates. Although security and truancy concerns may sometimes limit indoor-outdoor connections, it is nevertheless a good idea to open the doors completely when the weather permits. Not only is it healthier for students to breathe fresh air, but the open atmosphere also reduces energy consumption and extends opportunities for learning beyond the classroom.

of every child's education can work closely with educators to design suitable outdoor learning environments.

Students in the Environment Club at Scott Creek Primary School in Adelaide, Australia, have developed a nature discovery trail in an adjacent forest (or *bushland*, as it's referred to locally), for other students as well as members of the local community. Each station on the trail explores an element of the bushland, sharing facts about the location and explaining the group's replanting project.

Fieldwork tends to be quite active, not sedentary. As such, it can be supported in all but the most hostile climates, on all but the hottest or coldest 10 percent of days.

Designing for "Inside Goes Outside"

The inside-goes-outside learning modality is what generally springs to mind when you think of an outdoor classroom. It involves sitting, reading, reflecting, writing, drawing, chatting, and eating. Think fine motor activities rather than gross motor ones. Think formal and informal presentations. Think tables, chairs, benches, stages, and steps. Because reading, reflecting, making presentations, and so forth,

FIGURE 7.6 *Designing for "Inside Goes Outside"* A variety of outdoor seating options encourages students to read and study in the fresh air and sunshine.

are more sedentary, they aren't suitable activities for the outdoors all year round in all climates. However, I argue that outdoor learning areas are well worth investing in, in all but the coldest places on earth. Many schools in Helsinki, Finland, where the average maximum temperature is forty-eight degrees Fahrenheit, have outdoor seating. Presumably, the students aren't out there for long periods on the coldest days, and the kids bundle up when they do go outside, but the Finns' example shows that those of us living in milder climes could definitely make use of these kinds of facilities, too! In hot climates, it's also possible to make the most of the outdoors, which can be very comfortable with a little thought put to the design of the outdoor space.

Amphitheaters. Amphitheaters are another indoor-goes-outdoor modality setting, but they can also be used for play (in both the formal theatrical sense and the informal sense). A wonderful, multipurpose asset for a campus, amphitheaters can be very large spaces or quite intimate spaces for a very small group. Small

FIGURE 7.7 This terrace just outside a learning community is used both for relaxed activities like reading and lunch and for hands-on student project work.

FIGURE 7.8 *Before:* Middle school at Hillel Academy of Tampa, Florida. The windows have little view, and there is no direct access to outdoor areas.

FIGURE 7.9 *After:* The area was changed by the addition of large windows and doors, a wood deck, and outdoor furniture. This deck was subsequently shaded over with a fabric awning to extend its use during the day.

FIGURE 7.10 *Before:* This small green area between the elementary school and the library at Hillel Academy had limited access and was completely unused.

FIGURE 7.11 *After:* This same area redesigned as a learning terrace. It is opened up to a new commons area within the school and to the library and can be used as an outdoor reading and work area.

amphitheaters can be as simple as a single curved bench seat in a garden wall. Large amphitheaters, such as the Scott Arboretum Amphitheater at Swarthmore College, can be awe-inspiring places that are destinations in their own right.

Learning Terraces. *Learning terrace* is a term commonly applied to a breakout space outdoors, adjacent to a classroom, learning studio, or learning community, with a door connecting the two and ample windows for visual connection. The connection is important because it allows some students to work inside, some to work outside, and a teacher or teachers to supervise all the students, indoors and outdoors. If the terrace isn't located where it can be easily supervised, it's unlikely to be used for learning at all, as teachers won't allow their students to work there.

Successful learning terraces contain some furniture for students to sit and work at—a table for four is a good standard with which to begin, but it can be supplemented by other suitable outdoor elements such as round bistro tables and picnic tables. When selecting furniture for outdoor terraces, you may come across the question of how to secure it, particularly if your campus is open. Municipal-park-style fixed table and bench combinations reduce the comfort, flexibility, and creativity factor, but also the potential for vandalism from outside the school community. On balance, therefore, fixed pieces are often a preferred option.

The location of a learning terrace is also important. In the Northern Hemisphere, the southern side of a building is likely to offer gentle sunlight all day. In warmer climates, learning terraces are more likely to be used when they are under shade. Ceiling fans can be used to great effect and extend the times of the day when outdoor areas can be used.

CHAPTER EIGHT

From Cafeterias to Cafés

Celebrating Community

HUMAN BEINGS LIKE to congregate and socialize around food and beverages. At school, this natural human inclination to make eating a social activity gets distorted. Instead, we have created the equivalent of feeding stations, where the logistics of feeding X number of students in Y minutes drives all decisions about design.[1]

Neither the six educational strategies nor the four design principles are anywhere in evidence in the way that a majority of school cafeterias are designed. This chapter will look at how the design and redesign of school cafeterias can directly support all six strategies. A cafeteria designed to support student-centered learning would, for example, enable students to use the space for individual study and team collaboration by being available throughout the school day. Technology integration would allow students unfettered access to a wireless network for class projects and Internet research. Flexible scheduling would allow students to eat on demand as opposed to being given a time slot when they are required to eat. Well-designed cafeterias would facilitate teacher collaboration by having sections where teachers could meet in teams or even work with students. Cafeterias are also excellent places for community events and for connecting with nature via outdoor terraces and gardens.

The above educational strategies will be better met if the design also meets the four design principles so that it (1) is welcoming, (2) is versatile, (3) supports specific

A Variety of seating to support different groupings and activities

B Facilities for students to engage in the culinary arts

C Direct access to the outdoor dining and kitchen dining

D Kitchen garden adjacent to eating and food preparation spaces

FIGURE 8.1 Some Features of a Welcoming Cafeteria

learning activities, and (4) sends positive messages about identity and behavior. Let's look at the details that will ensure we meet all four design criteria.

MAKING STUDENTS FEEL WELCOME

Think about your favorite cafés. I'm not talking about school cafeterias here. I mean the places you like to go to for coffee or lunch. What is it about these places that you enjoy? Here's my personal list—yours might differ slightly.

- High-quality, fresh food and drinks
- Personal service—the staff know me by name
- A sunny aspect with seats by the windows, particularly important in winter
- A place to sit outside, which still feels like it is very much a part of the café
- Comfortable chairs (including a couch) and tables
- Cozy nooks to sit in, where I can see who's coming in and going out
- A place to plug my laptop in
- Free Wi-Fi

- Aesthetically pleasing interior design: interesting art on the walls, a variety of interesting lighting fixtures, and no ugly, institutional posters
- A small space to make me feel welcome, as though I am in a house rather than a barn, and to impart a feeling of exclusivity

Imagine you are the new owner of a café in your school's district. You need to put a lot of thought into marketing your café to attract local, regular customers. This is the mind-set needed for designing welcoming cafeterias.

A school could make its cafeteria more welcoming in a number of ways. The furniture could be changed from institutional tables for very large groups to a mix of tables for different-sized groupings. Other changes could involve the addition of soft colors and improved lighting and acoustics. A larger space could be broken up into smaller, cozier sections—with each section perhaps decorated with a different theme. Furniture sized for children helps them to feel welcome. If your school cafeteria caters for children of different ages and sizes, why not choose furniture that makes them all feel welcome?

Particularly in an elementary school setting, but potentially in all school settings, it makes sense for the cafeteria to be a welcoming space for parents and teachers as well as students. Comfortable couches can be a place for children and parents to read with one another before or during school hours. PTA events can also be held in the cafeteria.

ENSURING VERSATILITY

Typically, school cafeterias are designed on the assumption that all students need to eat in the same place, which is rarely actually the case. It also makes little sense to have a dedicated cafeteria space that is only used for two to three hours each day, and not at all for student learning. This idle space is a very poor return on investment, even if your school is blessed with the funds to provide it.

In a relatively primitive attempt to make these large, idle spaces more versatile, cafeteria furniture is often of the style that can be packed up and stored away to create a large, furniture-free space for assemblies, games, and similar activities (the multipurpose area is often known as a cafegymnatorium). This arrangement makes for a flexible space, but one that consequently often plays neither of its two roles particularly well. The necessary collapsible furniture makes table groupings too large since the tables seat between eight and twelve students, and the seating isn't comfortable enough to sit on for a decent period of time. Moreover, when the tables and chairs are packed away, they still take up lots of space.

Consider cafeterias as places in which a range of learning activities can happen without significant adjustment of furniture. Traditional whole-school cafeterias are too big for this multipurpose approach to work really well. A better alternative is to establish a number of smaller cafés around the campus, each catering to no more than 120 students, and preferably fewer. This setup will help make the spaces more versatile, as they can be used by students, teachers, and parents at other times. A change on this scale is most easily accomplished if you are designing a school campus from scratch, but as this chapter will show, more modest changes can be made on an incremental basis. See the sidebar "Do Now: How to Improve a Standard Cafeteria" for a range of ideas, from simple and inexpensive to more substantial.

From One Cafeteria to Many Cafés

Doing away altogether with the single cafeteria and replacing it with smaller café spaces scattered around the campus can solve many problems of the multifunction

FIGURE 8.2 Here, a satellite café doubles as a small commons and contains all the comforts of an upscale coffee shop.

DO NOW: HOW TO IMPROVE
A STANDARD CAFETERIA

Depending on the scope of resources available to you, you might be able to do some of the following to your standard cafeteria, starting with the easiest and ending with the most difficult changes:

- During mealtimes, set the tables with large pieces of blank paper (to draw on) as tablecloths, a small basket in the center of each table for cutlery, salt and pepper, and napkins, and even a little fresh flower—perhaps from the student-run kitchen garden (see the sidebar "Smart Idea: Kitchen Gardens").
- Allow the students to use the cafeteria during class time for group project meetings and individual study.
- Provide several picnic blankets for students to take outside and "picnic on" or to simply sit on while they work outside during good weather.
- Set up a small bookshelf in the cafeteria with secondhand books that can be exchanged, copies of the day's newspapers, and any appropriate magazines for the age group. Don't fret about the books disappearing (buy secondhand, and encourage students to return either the book they borrowed or an equivalent book from home). A wise principal once said he would be delighted if all of the books in the library were stolen, because it demonstrated children's love of the written word.
- Have students participate in the operation of the café. Participation can take the form of anything and everything, from clearing tables to growing produce for consumption in the café, to deciding on menu items, to cooking the food themselves. School personnel often begin pointing out all the barriers to implementing this change when we suggest it, but many schools are doing this successfully all over the world.
- Change the configuration of the existing furniture so that each table grouping is smaller (options of between two and six people per table).
- Make the entrance to the café feel homey with coat hooks and art on the walls, and a coir mat for dusting off shoes.
- Replace the furniture, getting inspiration from public cafés and restaurants rather than picking from your school supplier catalog. Secondhand furniture may be an option to consider. Choose a variety of soft seating and tables and chairs.
- Booth-style seating against interior cabinetry can give a sense of privacy while still allowing for supervision. Keep cabinets low, and use the space above them for glassed-in display of 3-D student work.
- Redecorate the space with a variety of lighting fixtures, different paint, or wallpaper to create a variety of different nooks and themed sections.
- Improve the natural lighting in the café by enlarging the windows.
- Improve the indoor-outdoor connection by replacing small doors with large sliding or garage-style glass doors that open to a terrace with seating outside.

cafeteria space. A central kitchen can cook food for all the cafés, but there is no need for all the students to eat centrally if dining amenities are spread around the campus.

A campus comprising several learning communities has a natural series of separate communities for food service as well. Separate learning community cafés can cater only for members of its own community, giving users a greater sense of ownership of the space. Also, because of its proximity to the community's teaching and learning spaces, the café can easily be used as an informal learning space, a community meeting place, or a breakout space. Just as commercial cafés are often located at the entrance to office buildings, where people can see each other entering and leaving the workplace, it makes sense to set up a dining space at the entry of each learning community.

Even if you don't have learning communities on your campus, a relatively low-cost option might be to renovate space for a café at each building entrance. In a cells-and-bells school, you could strategically choose a few classrooms throughout the campus, each adjacent to a hallway, an entry, or a stairwell, and remove the wall (between the hallway and the classroom). On the ground floor, the external wall could also be replaced with large glass doors and windows and a terrace or deck outside.

Admittedly, there are significant financial, architectural, and operational issues involved in this transition. For example, it is preferable to locate the satellite cafés where there is available running water. Nonetheless, it may be possible to reclaim space that's underused, such as corridor space, outdoor space, and classrooms that otherwise sit idle at lunchtime. Mobile food storage and heating units can transport food from a central kitchen to the satellite cafés. Turning one classroom in every five into a more open, commons-style lounge and dining room with permeable edges should be easy to do in most high schools without affecting scheduling—many classes can be held in this kind of space. And much of the old cafeteria space may be reclaimed for learning as well.

If staffing and supervision are issues, have students sign on to distribute each day's food to their home café, as they do at Harbor City International Charter School in Duluth, Minnesota. When each café includes space that teachers will want to hang out in as well, the chance to sit there with a colleague to eat lunch and keep an eye on students becomes a pleasure for teachers, not a chore.

Choose furniture that can be used by students doing independent study or small-group work, so that instead of being packed away after lunch, the furniture

FIGURE 8.3 At Cristo Rey Jesuit High School in Minneapolis, there is no central cafeteria; each floor has a serving area that's supplied from a central kitchen.

is simply used for learning activities. Furnishings should include soft seating as well as tables and chairs.

A great example of this kind of café arrangement is at Cristo Rey Jesuit High School in Minneapolis. A central kitchen prepares food for the students, who eat at four locations around the school. The students are served lunch in their own learning communities. The dining spaces are designed as multifunctional gathering areas adjacent to the community's classrooms. Included in these areas are various types of furniture, including small, high tables with bar stools; standard tables to seat four to six; and soft seating with low coffee tables. Also contained within the space are the students' lockers and access to all the classrooms and other learning spaces within the learning community; there are no corridors, so there is no wasted space.

If you are familiar with the concept of a learning community, you will see that having a café in each learning community helps give that community a sense of home. This is exactly how the cafés work at Cristo Rey.

FIGURE 8.4 While Sinarmas World Academy in Indonesia does have a central cafeteria (pictured), the school also has many smaller eating areas placed around the campus.

Sinarmas World Academy in Indonesia opted to retain the central cafeteria in its brand-new build (built in 2008), but also created smaller dining areas scattered throughout the campus. Because the students can eat their lunches in these small areas, closer to their home-base learning communities, there is room for most students in the school to dine at around the same time, without the pressure of taking a twenty-minute shift in the main cafeteria.

This concept of multiple cafés across a school campus is equally applicable to both full-service-lunch schools and those where students bring a packed lunch from home. At Duke School, an elementary and middle school in Durham, North Carolina, the students dine on food brought from home in their commons spaces. Australian schools have traditionally required students to bring their lunch from home. Students generally eat out in the playground (middle and high schools) or eat at their desks before going outside to play (elementary and middle schools). The versatility of multiple small cafés means many schools now have spaces for students

FIGURE 8.5 Students at Duke School in Durham bring their own lunches and eat them in this commons area.

to sit in comfort to eat. At the P. K. Yonge Developmental Research School at the University of Florida in Gainesville, the students are served from a central kitchen and eat at small group tables outdoors on good days or within their own learning communities on hot or rainy days.

SUPPORTING STUDENT LEARNING ACTIVITIES

School cafeterias typically take up a lot of space, which is by and large not used for educational purposes. Their design is more like that of a formal restaurant. In a restaurant, you are inclined to feel odd, first, if you are not eating and, second, if you are not in a group. In city cafés, however, it's common to see people working and reading, using their laptops or notepads. The design and operational cues of cafés suggest that you are welcome to eat, drink, or simply sit with an empty coffee cup in front of you, and to do so by yourself or in a group. Traditional school cafeterias don't have these same café-style operational cues in their design, but the cues aren't difficult to replicate in the school setting. And what an important message to send to school students: "Here is a place you should feel comfortable enough to study in."

Moving the cafeteria function into smaller cafés around the school will help make the dining space double up as learning space. Cafés like these are best located in areas that are easily supervised and adjacent to scheduled class space.

Even if you must continue to use one central cafeteria, you can use it to support specific learning activities. At the very least, you can allow teachers to bring classes in for activities that don't work so well in classroom spaces, like role-plays

FIGURE 8.6 The cafeteria at New Tech High @ Coppell in Texas is like a drop-in café. Open all day, it functions as another learning space for student project teams. Local businesspeople often visit the school to mentor students, and the adults and kids use the café space to work together over brown-bag lunches.

or debates. The cafeteria also works well for team teaching, where two or more teachers and their allocated students can work together in a larger space. Branson School in Marin, California, kept a single central cafeteria in its new build, but this area is open to students all day for study and social purposes. While an open, central cafeteria may have supervision implications that don't exist in the satellite model, such an arrangement still means the space is used all day, not just at lunchtime.

Many elements at Branson School underscore the four design principles. Most notable are the glass walls and garage doors that make the most of the building's green setting, eliminate the "corridor cram" when students are coming in and out in large numbers, and invite students to sit outside when the weather is fine. Café tables designed for four to six students keep the conversational groups small. Photovoltaic cells on the roof of this building allow the school to produce its own electricity and contributed to its LEED Platinum certification.

Another way to offer students very powerful, authentic learning experiences is to give them roles in the operation of the cafeteria (see, for example, the sidebar "Case Study: David Thompson Secondary School"). Almost every aspect of cafeteria operation can involve students of a particular age, to a certain extent. From the age of five, students can be expected to clear their place at the table, and they can participate in menu-planning. From seven, they can set tables and advertise special cafeteria- or café-based events. From ten, they can serve others, help with cleaning, and begin to understand the economics of the cafeteria's operation. From twelve, they can help with food preparation. (In some states, a certificate in food handling may be required. Perhaps students can complete the certificate for school credit.) Senior students can participate at a high level in the café's operation, potentially for credit toward their graduation.

From Prepackaged to Garden Fresh

Examples of students participating in food preparation with learning in mind are numerous and, with the right support, highly successful. The Alexander Kitchen Garden Foundation (Australia) supports schools in establishing learning programs for eight- to twelve-year-olds. The programs are based on the concept of growing, harvesting, preparing, and sharing fresh, seasonal food together, so that students participate in the entire food preparation cycle.[2]

What do gardens have to do with cafeterias? The answer to this question is, "In most cases, not enough." For many reasons, it makes sense for schools to have kitchen gardens. First, the gardens can provide fresh produce for students to eat on

CASE STUDY:
DAVID THOMPSON SECONDARY SCHOOL

Since 1994, David Thompson Secondary School has run a chef training program, where students prepare lunch for the whole school. From 2009 on, the program has also included a kitchen gardening component using the school's greenhouse, and the school has developed a strong culture of healthy eating. Here is a description of the program by Alison Bell, chef instructor at the school:

> Located in the scenic town of Invermere, British Columbia, Canada, David Thompson Secondary School is fortunate to have a unique and highly successful Professional Cooking program. Student chefs have more than their hands full—they run the school's cafeteria! Not your average school cafeteria, The *Rocky Mountain Café* features Canadian regional cuisine, multicultural menus, and organic and locally grown foods.
>
> At DTSS we strive to provide healthful foods to our staff and students. Our school is free of both "food" vending machines and deep-fried foods and The Rocky Mountain Café is recognized around the province as a leader for its innovative and healthful food. Like all teenagers, our students are inundated with junk food advertising, but our approach has had a positive influence on their food choices. Initially, this took a little educating! But with perseverance, we now have very food-savvy customers. Cedar Plank Wild Salmon with Wild Rice and Cranberry Chutney sells out in a flash. As does Curried Yam Bisque, Fresh Fruit and Yogurt Smoothies, Tofu Burritos, and whole-grain baked goods, just to name a few! All this while learning the fundamentals of food preparation in culinary courses or by completing the provincial Cook Level One qualification.
>
> Since the inception of the program in 1994, we have worked to instil a respect for food in our students and the greater school community. In addition, we do all we can to bring an awareness of the social issues surrounding food and food security to our students. For example, we prepare frozen meals for the Food Bank, hold a "Hunger Banquet" on World Food Day, have established strong farm-to-school alliances with local producers and host the senior citizens of our community at special catered events. Every Tuesday, we hold a Slow Food Cooking Club after school, which is sponsored by Slow Food Columbia Valley. Best of all, since April 2009, we have been growing food for our program in the Community Greenhouse at DTSS.*

Even if it is only possible for one small senior hospitality class, one day per week, to help in or even run the kitchen, that is an opportunity realized. Look for the closest links with the curriculum across the school, and begin there.

*David Thomson Secondary School, "Chef Training," school web page, David Thompson Secondary School, Invermere, British Columbia, accessed January 29, 2014, www.sd6.bc.ca/dtss/course_outlines/chef%20training/intro%20page.htm.

site, reducing the environmental impact of the cafeteria or cafés. Second, kitchen gardens are excellent resources for authentic learning across the curriculum, with potential applications not only in health and science but also in literacy and numeracy. Finally, the learning opportunities afforded by a garden cannot be overstated. Learning about where food comes from in a textbook is beaten hands-down by the experience of growing and preparing your own food to eat. See the sidebar "Smart Idea: Kitchen Gardens" for more illustrations of the benefits of school gardens.

People often assume that kitchen gardens are only possible at schools with abundant open green space. That is not true. Kitchen gardens can be started in simple wooden crates set up on hardscape surfaces and even on school roofs. The materials needed to start a kitchen garden can often be donated by your local hardware store. No school is too big or too small to afford a kitchen garden.

In Australia, celebrity chef and author of arguably the country's most highly regarded cookbook, *The Cook's Companion*, Stephanie Alexander has developed a holistic program for students aged eight to twelve. The program teaches the students about healthy eating by having them participate in growing, harvesting, preparing, and sharing food at school. Alexander's book *Kitchen Garden Cooking with Kids* (2008) provides a detailed, practice-based guide to establishing and working with kitchen gardens on school campuses. For more information, see Stephanie Alexander's Kitchen Garden Foundation (www.kitchengardenfoundation.org.au).

ELICITING POSITIVE BEHAVIORS

The challenge of converting an institutional cafeteria to a learning-friendly one can become an interesting student project, which generates a sense of ownership by the student community and in turn an increased respect for the space. Many of the earlier suggestions in this chapter can be implemented by the students themselves, with the express permission and guidance of staff. Students should be consulted in the design process. Beyond better furnishings, color, acoustics, and lighting, students could participate in planning healthy menus that they could then help prepare in the kitchen. Students could also help to start and maintain a kitchen garden. If funds allow, students could help with the creation of a series of smaller cafés with warming pantries (in larger schools) so that the eating function starts to become decentralized and less institutional.

Schools can encourage positive behaviors by implementing many of the principles of welcoming, versatile, learning-focused café space.

SMART IDEA: KITCHEN GARDENS

A kitchen garden in school has many benefits. It teaches children about the biology of plants through actual, hands-on work. It involves healthy, outdoor physical activity where children breathe clean air. A garden raises awareness about health and nutrition, and children's involvement with a garden teaches them about the differences between mass-produced, chemically treated, and genetically modified foods and organically grown local produce. From an early age, children who work in a garden can cultivate a taste for healthy fruits and vegetables. A kitchen garden can also spur interest in cooking healthy meals. The benefits of kitchen gardens are so numerous that schools should do their best to start one, even if they only have a small piece of land available for the purpose. In fact, even in dense urban areas where land is at a premium, schools should consider installing a rooftop kitchen garden.

FIGURES 8.7 AND 8.8 The Groundswell Community Greenhouse and Permaculture Gardens, along with its partner organization, Groundswell Network Society, of Invermere British Columbia, has created a permaculture garden beside this greenhouse; students provide food for the local community here.

FIGURE 8.9 Collingwood College in Melbourne, Australia, pioneered the Stephanie Alexander Kitchen Garden project, where children have the opportunity to plant, grow, harvest, cook, and eat organic foods.

FIGURE 8.10 At the Anne Frank Inspire Academy, set to open in San Antonio in 2014, a vegetable garden is a key site feature. Work in the garden will be integrated into the curriculum, and food grown by students will be prepared in the school kitchen.

Putting Theory into Practice
Where Should Schools Begin?

BUILDING UPON THE rationale for redesigning twenty-first-century schools and successful examples of schools that are using facilities design to address twenty-first-century education goals, this chapter answers two questions. First, what steps can schools take to ensure that the design principles discussed throughout this book are implemented to create effective schools? And second, how do schools get started? Several case studies in this chapter discuss how various communities dealt with the challenge of aligning school buildings with educational aspirations. Not all schools will start the process flush with cash to do facilities improvements. In fact, despite the fact that billions of dollars will be spent each year on school building and refurbishment projects, most schools have very modest budgets allocated for school facility improvements. That is all the more reason why school and district personnel need to follow a thoughtful process that maximizes the educational value of their facilities investments.

STARTING WITH INCREMENTAL CHANGE

Very often, the educational transformation facilitated by school building improvements begins with small changes that are faster, easier, and less expensive to implement than a major modernization of the entire school campus. Smaller pilot projects may include no more than 150 students and six to seven teachers within a fully redesigned small learning community. Pilots can then be scaled up at a pace that the school community can handle until a whole school is functioning according to the new paradigm in fully renovated facilities.

School facilities changes should be done with the future in mind since they are relatively expensive and usually last a long time. However, it is also important that the changes don't get too far ahead of where the teachers at a particular school might be.

The ideas contained in this book can work for schools no matter where they are on the change continuum. Schools that are just starting the journey might invest in the improvement of an entryway to make the school more welcoming using some of the ideas listed in chapter 2. Other schools might tackle a small wing of the school to reclaim hallway space, and yet others might create a learning suite by opening up the wall between two classrooms and adding an adjacent learning terrace. In other words, schools can start the change process by selectively taking ideas

FIGURE C.1 Simple changes in furnishings like bringing in modular tables can jump-start your efforts to create a learning building.

from the various chapters in this book and applying them to small pilot projects before taking the bigger leap of whole school transformation.

IMPORTANCE OF PROFESSIONAL DEVELOPMENT AND CHANGED PEDAGOGY

Smaller design changes whose ultimate goal is to improve teachers' practices are far more likely to be successfully implemented than design changes that focus merely on the building. Ideally, for changes to school facilities such as those described throughout this book to succeed, they must be accompanied by changes in teaching practices, school structures, and even student assessment.

Teachers aiming to change their teaching methods and practices might, for example, act more like facilitators; make learning become more student-directed; ensure that content serves as a catalyst for higher-level thinking; offer students more in-depth learning experiences, more interdisciplinary work, and more project work. Additionally, technology may need to be freed from computer labs and become ubiquitous, and teachers will need to collaborate more and be given more time for lesson planning. Of course, such changes may require a complete makeover of the school schedule, including doing away with bells altogether, and, more importantly, a strong commitment to providing teachers with needed professional development.

ASSESSMENT OF EXISTING SPACES

The alignment of school building spaces with pedagogical needs begins with an assessment of existing facilities. Traditional school building assessments are one-dimensional in that they tend to focus on the physical condition of the building such as the integrity of roofs and mechanical and electrical systems as opposed to the educational adequacy of the school facility for the delivery of a twenty-first-century education. In appendixes A and B, I have provided two very different checklists, one for elementary school facilities and one for secondary school facilities. These checklists represent a hybrid tool based on Lorraine Maxwell's "Classroom Assessment Scale" and Fielding Nair International's "Educational Facilities Effectiveness Instrument."[1] Schools should begin by using these checklists for a quick and accurate assessment of their school facility's effectiveness as a place to deliver a twenty-first-century education. Where multiple schools are involved, then at a minimum, a representative sample of schools should be evaluated. These checklists are also valuable because they provide educators and laypersons on the team with a tool to measure the quality of architectural designs that are created to upgrade or replace older facilities. Naturally, every effort must be made to ensure that the selected design scores as close to the maximum on the list as possible.

A DISCOVERY PROCESS TO DEVELOP A FACILITIES MASTER PLAN

For larger projects—whether they run $100,000 or $100 million—you must begin with a rigorous discovery process containing several discrete steps to ensure a meaningful, sustainable change. Here are some elements of a typical discovery process:

- Orientation meeting with the principal and school leadership team (SLT)
- Site walk with school custodian and some members of the SLT to get a firsthand look at the opportunities and constraints of the campus
- Visioning workshop with the SLT to agree on a long-range vision that the facilities improvements must support
- Community workshop at which all school stakeholders, including students, teachers, parents, education and business leaders, and government representatives, will be invited
- Teacher workshop to discuss new curriculum, pedagogies, and scheduling and the spaces needed to support them
- Ethos and environmental sustainability workshop to ensure that all changes respect the school culture and ethos and are consistent with the school's commitment to environmental sustainability

The purpose of the discovery process is to end up with a specific master plan to serve as a blueprint for action. The master plan will provide a vision for the school as a whole and contain a prioritized list of both short- and long-term recommendations for change. It will also include budget estimates for what each recommended change will cost.

ESTABLISHING A LEADERSHIP TEAM

There are two key reasons why the discovery process should be collaborative, preferably under the guidance of a leadership team. First, the voices of all key education stakeholders must be heard and their needs met. Second, buy-in from a large cross-section of the school community will be critical as the school seeks support for funding the needed improvements.

Individual superintendents and school principals tend to relegate matters related to school facilities to their in-house engineering professionals. This is a mistake. Facilities people are great when it comes to managing the day-to-day affairs of the school physical plant but they may not have the expertise to consider the effect of design on pedagogy, and vice versa. For this reason, a school project should begin with the appointment of a leadership team whose size and composition would vary with the scope and scale of the project.

Generally, for districtwide master plans, large renovations, school additions, or new-school projects, a leadership team should be large enough to include as many key stakeholders as possible but small enough to be effective. I have worked on projects where leadership teams had representatives from the district, school management, or both (like the superintendent or principal) plus respected teachers, parents, students, community representatives, and local business leaders. Ideally, the leadership teams should not exceed ten to twelve people. To avoid the complications of creating a new legal entity, the teams should be volunteer bodies that only have the authority to make recommendations. The legally responsible school executives and school boards can use these recommendations to craft their own decisions. While leadership teams may not have any official standing, their work will carry weight with the community because they take into consideration the opinions and wishes of all education stakeholders.

IMPORTANCE OF HIRING A PROFESSIONAL TEAM EARLY

Avoid the temptation to define your project too early in the process. Often, school leaders will have a strong idea about what they want and then go through the motions to rationalize their decisions afterward. In fact, most school facilities projects in the United States are already fully defined in terms of scope and budget before facilities professionals have even been hired. The better approach is to write a very generic scope of work for the facilities professional. The document should talk generally about the school or district's aspirations and briefly describe the project and budget that can be used to solicit proposals from interested teams of school facility planners and architects.

Schools and school districts make few decisions that have more long-term influence on the lives of hundreds if not thousands of students than the decision to hire a facilities planner or architect. That is why it is imperative to make this decision carefully and thoughtfully. Your selected design professional will lead you through the steps in the discovery process discussed above.

LESSONS FROM THE FIELD

The following case studies illustrate the influence that facilities wield in changing the dominant teacher-centered educational paradigm to a more student-centered one. While the buildings themselves are only one piece of the change process, they become a powerful, visible symbol of a new way to deliver education.

Don't Wait for the Big Money: Middletown Public Schools, Middletown, Rhode Island

At around three thousand students, Middletown Public Schools is a fairly typical US school district. In 2006, the district decided to take stock of its aging school facilities. A comprehensive assessment of its five school campuses (three elementary schools, one middle school, and one high school) told a story that is repeated in districts around the country; all the schools had aged to the point where they no longer met the demands of a twenty-first-century education. In response to these findings, the school district commissioned a master plan to determine what it would take to upgrade or replace the schools to twenty-first-century standards. The price tag of $121 million contained in the 2007 master plan was staggering and, realistically, beyond the capacity of this small middle-class town's ability to raise from its citizens. On the other hand, the option of doing nothing would mean that the community's schools would fall further into obsolescence and that, eventually, the town itself would suffer the consequences as parents exited the district in search of better schools.

Utilizing the condition assessment and educational adequacy data gathered during the master planning process, Middletown embarked on a program of incremental, low-budget pilot projects. The district focused on spending money in a manner that would yield the biggest educational bang for the buck.

The first project was Forest Avenue Elementary School, where a wing of the school housing the school's kindergarten and first-grade students was selected for a pilot renovation. The design of the new space was developed in close consultation with the teachers who would be assigned to the new space. It became immediately apparent that the best approach would be one that converted the wing into a small learning community with a variety of spaces, including a large commons area that captured the area previously used as a hallway. The learning community that was created as a result of the renovation was designed from the ground up according to the principles identified in this book—to be welcoming, to be versatile, to support multiple ways of learning, and to create a positive school climate.

At the direction of the district superintendent and the facilities director, conversations with the teachers focused on better ways to deliver education and how the new space could serve as a catalyst to change pedagogy. Of particular importance was the teachers' decision that they would like to work collaboratively rather than individually in classrooms as they had done before. Students would continue to be assigned to a homeroom teacher but would also have unfettered access to all the other teachers who worked in the community. The new arrangement offered students a great many more learning modalities than were possible in their old classroom setting; it also allowed for inter-age groupings and opportunities to base group size on what the children were learning and what individual children needed.

Middletown's first pilot project—the Forest Avenue Elementary School Early Learning Center—opened in 2008. It was built over one summer at a cost of about $180,000. Since its opening, the pilot has caught the attention of educators worldwide who are modeling their own teaching and learning practices according to what the teachers at this small Middletown school are doing. The success of the pilot has also spawned a total of five other pilot projects at various district schools, with costs varying from $90,000 to $320,000. These projects included an additional fourth- and fifth-grade learning community, an Internet café where an old library once existed, and a high school art center.

It's OK to Start Small: Hillel Academy of Tampa, Florida

When Amy Wasser, the principal of Hillel Academy (a preK–8 school of two hundred students), first started looking at the possibilities for improving the tired old school campus, she had a difficult time getting people to pay attention. After all, as a Blue Ribbon School of Excellence, the school seemed to have no compelling reason to spend money on the buildings. Consequently, she decided to start small. The first project at the school involved the opening up of two early-years classrooms to the outdoors to enable teachers in adjoining classrooms to work together and extend learning onto an outside paved area. The success of this initiative despite some early misgivings led to a fund-raising campaign for a larger project to renovate the entire elementary school building. At first, Wasser was simply looking to extend to the elementary school the kind of modest success she had enjoyed with the early-years classrooms. However, as we discussed the project, she saw how the entire wing of the school could be remodeled into a small learning community. Of course, this meant rethinking the way the elementary school operated from a traditional teacher-centered model to a student-centered model with a greater emphasis on project-based learning. Teacher collaboration was also greatly emphasized as a part of the transition to the learning-community model, and a well-outfitted teacher workroom was included in the renovation plan. This project was also completed successfully and was extremely well received by the whole community. After that, when the academy decided to renovate its middle school, with the goal of extending the student-centered model all the way through the eighth grade, funds became available more easily and the project was also completed on schedule and within budget.

Hillel Academy owes much of the success of its transformation into a twenty-first-century school to the academy's measured pace of change. The pace allowed teachers to become acquainted with the new pedagogies and practices that the renewed campus enabled. Professional development for teachers was also key, as was the support from the school's leadership. Parents and teachers were kept informed and involved throughout, and many were recruited to help directly with the project on assignments such as painting, installing carpet, and acquiring good-quality furniture at cost (from a parent who owned a local furniture store). Furniture manufacturers also provided several items free of charge since they realized that Hillel Academy would be a great venue to showcase their products and demonstrate how the companies supported twenty-first-century teaching and learning practices.

The entire school was renovated over three summers, and each project was accomplished for relatively small sums of money (around $250,000 each for complete renovations of the 10,000-square-foot elementary and middle schools). The amount is a fraction of what schools and school districts normally spend on their school facility projects without realizing the educational benefits that Hillel Academy realized.

Create a "Learning Lab" for Education Innovation: Horace Greeley High School, Chappaqua, New York

Horace Greeley High School is one of the nation's highest-performing schools. Its school facilities are antiquated by twenty-first-century standards, but they are in reasonably good condition and not crying out for renovation. Given these

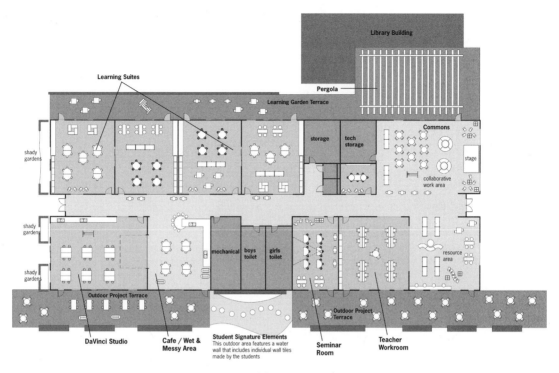

FIGURE C.2   Based on the success of the modest effort to open up classrooms to the outside, Hillel Academy undertook more ambitious projects such as this one to transform its intermediate wing (second to fifth grade) into a small learning community. The plan was modified during construction to eliminate the computer lab in favor of mobile computing throughout the learning community.

circumstances—a good education being delivered in acceptable facilities—Horace Greeley could have chosen to do nothing for at least the next few years. Instead, it has embraced the path of innovation designed to keep the school relevant and successful over the coming years.

In taking stock of its future, the leadership of Chappaqua Central School District and Horace Greeley decided that the school needed to move slowly away from a highly compartmentalized and departmentalized model of education, even though the model is practiced by a majority of high schools nationwide. In their

Before and After:
Forest Avenue Elementary School, Middletown, Rhode Island, and Hillel Academy of Tampa, Florida

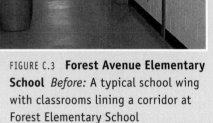

FIGURE C.3 **Forest Avenue Elementary School** *Before:* A typical school wing with classrooms lining a corridor at Forest Elementary School

FIGURE C.4 **Forest Avenue Elementary School** *After:* Removing walls and adding flexible furnishings in the same area created an early-learning center commons. The overall space has been designed as a small learning community, which has been operating successfully since 2008.

FIGURE C.5 **Hillel Academy** *Before:* This classroom at Hillel Academy had no outdoor connection and had poor views.

FIGURE C.6 **Hillel Academy** *After:* The outside wall of the same classroom was opened up with full-height sliding doors to connect to views and an outdoor learning terrace.

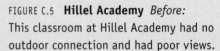

FIGURE C.7   The 4,000-square-foot learning lab at Horace Greeley High School in Chappaqua, New York was created in an area previously occupied by four classrooms and two small offices. The variety of spaces near one another enables a significantly larger number of teaching and learning modalities than would be permitted in a traditional classroom setting.

view, this model made it much more difficult for teachers to work collaboratively to create and deliver interdisciplinary courses. The school's physical setup of classrooms along corridors also limited the richness and variety of hands-on, student-led activities that was possible.

To move forward, Horace Greeley realized that two things needed to happen simultaneously. First, the teachers needed to be trained to work together and, with the help of outside professionals, to create and deliver new, interdisciplinary courses. These courses would be piloted on a relatively small scale before being scaled up. Second, the school needed a new space for these new courses—a place where students could access significantly more learning modalities than would be permitted in a traditional classroom setting.

In moving forward with these two priorities, the school established a core group of seventeen "innovation fellows"—a group of the school's teachers who volunteered to design and deliver the new curriculum. Simultaneously, the school hired an educational facility planner and educational consultant to help with both the curriculum design and the design of a pilot space in which the new curriculum could be delivered.

Given a very tight budget of under $200,000, including consulting fees, the school identified a small area of 4,000 square feet on the ground floor. This area, comprising four classrooms and a couple of offices, was to be converted into a learning lab for the use of the innovation fellows to deliver the newly developed interdisciplinary courses.

The design of the learning lab is similar in some ways to a small learning community, but unlike a small learning community, this space is designed for a specific group of teachers and as a location where these teachers can work collaboratively to deliver courses that would be impossible to deliver in their traditional classrooms. The philosophy behind the design is simple—create a space that will be comfortable and exciting and permit a far wider variety of teaching and learning activities than is currently possible elsewhere in the school. In keeping with the notion of a learning building, the space has sufficient variety and flexibility that it becomes a template for whatever teaching and learning activities need to happen at any given time. Thus, the area is not expected to look and feel the same (as classrooms tend to do) as the semester progresses, since the teachers and students who use the space (and not the architects who designed it) get to make the day-to-day decisions on how it will be used.

Community Involvement Works:
Bloomfield Hills High School, Bloomfield Hills, Michigan

At the height of the economic downturn in 2009, the community of Bloomfield Hills was facing shrinking enrollment, reduced budgets, and two fifty-year-old obsolete high school buildings with millions of dollars in needed capital improvements. Many proposals for fixing the problems were considered. The first involved the creation of two new and smaller schools at the location of the existing campuses. This proposal would have cost upward of $150 million and was defeated by the community in a bond referendum. The school district subsequently came up with another proposal, this time for one new high school that would consolidate the populations of both high schools at one site. This proposal, priced at $97 million, was also defeated in a bond referendum. Notably, neither of these proposals envisioned a significant departure from traditional school design.

By this time, the community was up in arms, urging the recall of the school board. There was a tremendous amount of bitterness about the whole high school mess, with mounting opposition to any major capital improvement program to fix the schools. A new superintendent, Rob Glass, was hired, and he immediately set about mending fences with the community. He established a leadership team, which included both proponents and opponents of a new high school. This team was first charged with the task of hiring a nationally reputed school planning and design firm with solid community building credentials.

The team's efforts to form a vision and a plan offer an excellent example of how a comprehensive discovery process, as described at the beginning of this chapter, works in practice. It began with a detailed facilities assessment followed by a leading practices workshop, where the community heard about success stories of school transformation from around the world. Next came several "fireside chats" to give small groups of community residents an opportunity to share their thoughts and ideas. Several online surveys and focus groups were conducted, and a new "hybrid" plan emerged as a result. This plan would preserve much of the existing high school, demolish portions that were dysfunctional, and build additions to create a brand-new, state-of-the-art 1,500-student Bloomfield Hills High School. The scale of the school would be broken down through the creation of eleven learning communities, none of which would exceed 150 students. The most important key to the success of the new plan was that it was seen as a way to upgrade not just the school facility but education itself. The community understood that redesigning its obsolete buildings could not only sustain the educational excellence its schools currently enjoyed, but also support growth in the community's property values.

Community support slowly built for the new hybrid plan, which was priced at $67 million—$30 million less than the last plan rejected by the community. When the proposal was put on the ballot once more in a special election during May 2012, it was approved by an overwhelming 61 percent majority, sweeping twenty-seven out of thirty precincts. The project started construction in 2013 and is expected to open in the fall of 2015.

This case study provides two important lessons. One, twenty-first-century schools do not have to cost more than traditional schools and can, in fact, be developed for substantially less money. Two, even at a time of fiscal austerity, communities will step up to the plate if they get the message that school facilities spending is not just about buildings but about a whole new way to educate their children for the twenty-first century.

A FINAL MESSAGE

The case studies discussed in this chapter represent a wide range of solutions to the problem of inadequate and outdated school facilities. They all share one common goal—to provide teachers and children with varied, comfortable learning environments in order to expand the range of available teaching and learning methods. Whatever the impetus for facilities improvements—be it a need to consolidate and upgrade buildings (e.g., Bloomfield Hills) or to change pedagogy (e.g., Hillel Academy), schools can do more with their capital dollars than simply repair what is broken or replace what is old. Most education leaders have already accepted the commonsense idea that educational practices need to keep up with the changes in the world outside school. Despite this imperative for change, leaders can see that the one element of the whole educational enterprise that has remained almost exactly as it did forty or even fifty years ago is the school building. Even when tens of millions of dollars are spent to renovate, add to, or build new school facilities, the results tend to mirror the predominant and familiar model of buildings with classrooms arrayed along a double-loaded corridor. This arrangement, unfortunately, severely limits the extent to which the best educational theory can actually be translated into practice. Especially in a traditional setting, teachers find it difficult to arrange for collaborative work, to organize students in inter-age groupings, and to create and deliver interdisciplinary courses. Similarly, traditional settings make it more difficult for students to work independently, conduct research, work on projects that require a hands-on approach, engage in peer tutoring, and so on. Educators routinely express their desire for these effective learning and teaching modalities—the very activities that this book promotes through targeted improvements to school facilities.

Putting logic aside for a moment, we cannot ignore the emotional component of school reform. I have often witnessed passionate arguments about what schools are supposed to look like and which educational practices work best. These emotional statements often trump the evidence in these areas. Change is difficult in all domains, but nowhere is it harder to implement than in the world of education. Take the simple matter of student comfort. Some parents still believe that giving students comfortable furnishings may militate against discipline and rigor, despite evidence to the contrary.

The recommendations in this book, taken together, call for schools to look and function in ways that many parents will find unfamiliar, and this alone would be a reason for them to be concerned. That is why school planners and architects need to expend a lot of effort discussing leading practices in education and school design, familiarizing school stakeholders with new educational methods and practices and the design of learning environments to support these new approaches.

This book brings under one roof many of the best ideas in education and architecture. I tried to make an effective case for the need to look at school facilities with the same critical eye that we look at education itself. Beyond that, it is my fervent hope that the specific strategies and suggestions this book contains will provide school leaders with the information they need to apply their ever-scarcer capital dollars toward facilities improvements that will result in meaningful and measurable educational outcomes.

Educational Effectiveness Survey

Elementary School Facilities

Instructions: Read each category, and fill in the box the number that best describes the school environment.★

Color, materials, and texture: ☐

2 = *Excellent:* There is variety in the color of walls, flooring, and furnishings without being overwhelming. Texture varies in more than two mediums (e.g., two or more types of flooring, two or more wall surfaces). The space provides opportunities for children to handle different sensory materials such as water and sand.

1 = *Adequate:* The materials and colors vary slightly and are soft and not overwhelming.

0 = *Inadequate:* The colors and materials are high contrast and overwhelming, and there is very little distinction between different displays and activity areas.

Social play space and materials: ☐

Space for groups to play together with manipulative materials; items that allow for children to create something of their choosing (e.g., Lego and other blocks, Play-Doh, figurines, cars, train tracks).

2 = *Excellent:* Enough space and materials for four or more children, in more than three locations within the principal learning area.

1 = *Adequate:* Enough space and materials for two or three children, in at least two locations.

0 = *Inadequate:* Not enough space or materials for more than two children to play together at the same time.

Scale: ☐

2 = *Excellent:* All space, furniture, and equipment are at age-appropriate scale and heights accommodating both students' and teachers' ergonomic needs; more than one permanent change in height of a physical structure, which a child can easily perceive (e.g., change in ceiling height, change in floor level, lofted space, ceiling-hung banners).

1 = *Adequate:* Most aspects of the space, furniture, and equipment are at the appropriate scale; and there is one change in height of physical structure (can be temporary or permanent).

0 = *Inadequate:* Scale and height of space, furnishings, and equipment are inappropriate for the age group or user needs, or focuses solely on the ergonomic needs of the teacher. There is no perceivable change of height within the space.

Personalization: ☐

2 = *Excellent:* Child-generated work is displayed and visibly accessible to children, and the work is individualized and original (not suspiciously perfect and all alike).

1 = *Adequate:* Mix of child-generated work and commercial posters are displayed at mostly appropriate heights but not *all* student's work is displayed.

0 = *Inadequate:* No child-generated work is visible, and any displays are adult generated or commercial posters.

Principal learning areas: ☐

2 = *Excellent:* The principal learning area allows for a variety of activities and includes a space for experimentation or messy work with adjacent cleanup facilities. Students have access to electronic and printed resources and project materials as well as prep and storage areas adjacent to work areas. There is ample space for all students and teachers to move around without congestion or awkward circulation.

1 = *Adequate:* There are cleanup facilities available only in specialized rooms, and the storage and prep areas are available to students during certain classes when they can be supervised. There is adequate space for almost all students to work actively and move around the room.

0 = *Inadequate:* There is little to no student access to resources and materials, and the storage areas are only for use by teachers. Cleanup facilities are not adjacent to project work areas. The space is limited and is problematic during active project working times.

Privacy: ☐

2 = *Excellent:* Space and furniture provide two or three spaces for children to feel a sense of privacy and to control their interaction with others (e.g., semi-enclosed spaces, nooks, dedicated furnishings, window seat for one or two children).

1 = *Adequate:* Children can find or create at least one space for privacy.

0 = *Inadequate:* There are no opportunities for children to find privacy.

Circulation and boundaries: ☐

2 = *Excellent:* Enough space between all or most activity areas to allow children to navigate the space without interrupting an ongoing activity; clear distinctions between all or most activity areas (e.g., visual separation, arrangement of furniture, rug, change in color or materials).

1 = *Adequate:* Enough circulation space around some of the activity areas; limited enclosure or distinction between activity areas.

0 = *Inadequate:* Little or no circulation space between areas as described above; no distinctions between activity areas.

Ownership: ☐

2 = *Excellent:* Three or more areas that each student can call his or her own (e.g., cubbies, mats, seat at table, pillow).

1 = *Adequate:* One or two spaces that children can call their own.

2 = *Inadequate:* No spaces that children can call their own.

Restorative spaces: ☐

To combat cognitive fatigue, children need opportunities to engage in activities that do not require focused attention. Spaces for these restorative activities, such as watching birds at a feeder, should be accessible, where children can go on their own. Restorative spaces should contain items such as soft furnishings, plants, animals, a window seat, or an aquarium that are easy to access or view.

2 = *Excellent:* Three or more restorative spaces in the principal learning area.

1 = *Adequate:* One or two restorative spaces.

0 = *Inadequate:* No restorative spaces available.

Variety and flexibility of space: ☐

2 = *Excellent:* A variety of materials, furniture, and equipment that allows students to change how the space looks and is used (e.g., build or create spaces, move furnishings, change a presentation area into an informal breakout space, display their own work); also a variety in types and sizes of spaces.

1 = *Adequate:* One or two opportunities for students to change how the spaces looks or is used.

0 = *Inadequate:* Little to no opportunity for students to change how the space looks or is used.

Gross motor skills area: ☐

2 = *Excellent:* A dedicated indoor play area available for all children to use daily; a dedicated outdoor play area for gross motor activity.

1 = *Adequate:* An indoor space that can be made available for gross motor activity during the day; also possibly a dedicated outdoor area.

0 = *Inadequate:* No adequate spaces for gross motor activity.

Storage: ☐

2 = *Excellent:* Mostly all materials and toys are stored in a way that is accessible for all children (e.g., containers are small enough for small children to reach and carry themselves so as to not depend on adults for access).

1 = *Adequate:* Some materials and toys, but not all, are stored in ways that are accessible to all children.

0 = *Inadequate:* Most materials and toys are stored in a way that is not accessible to all children.

Teachers as professionals: ☐

2 = *Excellent:* Teachers workspaces are clustered together in small teams sharing a professional workroom with computers, phones, and other equipment. This space provides both formal and informal meeting spaces and is equipped with tools for collaborating and planning. The workroom is adjacent to principal learning areas and allows for passive supervision of the learning community.

1 = *Adequate:* Teachers share a semiprivate office. There is a common teacher workroom with necessary equipment accessible, but there is limited opportunity for informal and formal meeting and planning.

0 = *Inadequate:* Each teacher is isolated in his or her own classroom, with limited connectivity to other teachers for collaborating, planning, and socializing.

Lighting: ☐

2 = *Excellent:* Several types of lighting and the opportunity to vary it; easy ways to control levels of lighting (e.g., dimmers, shades); access to natural daylight.

1 = *Adequate:* No dimmers or other lighting controls, but a variety of lighting fixtures; some access to natural daylight.

0 = *Inadequate:* No opportunity to change the level of lighting; no variety in lighting; little access to natural daylight.

Furniture: ☐

2 = *Excellent:* There is a variety of furniture, which is easy to use and move and in good repair. The scale is age-appropriate.

1 = *Adequate:* There is some variety; furniture is in good repair and is mostly age-appropriate in scale.

0 = *Inadequate:* The furniture is not in good repair and is not the appropriate scale.

Technology: ☐

2 = *Excellent:* Children can access Internet-connected devices from any location with all-campus wireless networking for anytime, anywhere learning.

1 = *Adequate:* Students can access Internet-connected computers during most of the day.

0 = *Inadequate:* Technology is limited to centralized and static computer labs or computers at the back of the classroom. There is little or no wireless connectivity.

Score Card ☐

Add up the scores for each category: ☐

20–32 = *Excellent:* High effectiveness in supporting twenty-first-century learning.

10–19 = *Adequate:* Acceptable performance in supporting twenty-first-century learning, but there is room for improvement.

0–10 =   *Inadequate:* An urgent need for change to support twenty-first-century learning.

Source: Adapted from classroom rating scale in Lorraine Maxwell, "Competency in Child Care Settings: The Role of the Physical Environment," *Environment and Behavior* 22, no. 10 (2006); and the EFEI (Educational Facilities Effectiveness Instrument), by FNI. © Fielding Nair International.

Educational Effectiveness Survey

Middle and High School Facilities

Instructions: Read each category, and fill in the box the number that best describes the school environment.★

Color, materials, and texture: ☐

2 = *Excellent:* There is variety in the color of walls, flooring, and furnishings without being overwhelming. Texture varies in more than two mediums (e.g., two or more types of flooring, two or more wall surfaces).

1 = *Adequate:* The materials and colors vary slightly and are soft and not overwhelming.

0 = *Inadequate:* The colors and materials are high contrast and overwhelming, and there is very little distinction between different displays and activity areas.

Acoustics: ☐

2 = *Excellent:* Background noise is low, and there is an acceptable level of classroom "buzz." Noise is absorbed by soft fixtures and furnishings. Appropriate layouts so that loud areas are not located near quiet spaces.

1 = *Adequate:* Low level of background noise, but appropriate adjacencies have been created to ensure that loud activity areas are not located near quiet spaces.

0 = *Inadequate:* Noise and echoing is distracting, and activity areas with different sound-level requirements are placed near one another. Because of the lack of good acoustic design, the fear of making too much noise often limits the students' freedom to collaborate and actively work on projects.

Home base and individual storage: ☐

2 = *Excellent:* Students have personal workstations with lockable storage that they are permitted to personalize and are responsible for maintaining. Project materials, resources, and tools are readily available to all students and are located adjacent to the appropriate project prep and work areas.

1 = *Adequate:* Workstations are shared and are not personalized to each student. Each student does have his or her own personal lockable storage space, and community-shared material and project storage space is adjacent to appropriate spaces, but is not accessible to all students.

0 = *Inadequate:* Students are not provided with a personal workstation or a lockable storage area. Most project materials, resources, tools, etc., are either not available or stored in a way that is not accessible to students.

Personalization and display: ☐

2 = *Excellent:* Student-generated work is displayed and visibly accessible to students, faculty, and visitors, and the work is individualized and original (not suspiciously perfect and all alike).

1 = *Adequate:* Mix of varied and original student-generated work and commercial posters are displayed, but not *all* student's work is displayed.

0 = *Inadequate:* No student-generated work is visible, and any displays are commercial posters, *or* only the "top" students' work is displayed, and the work is unoriginal.

Technology: ☐

2 = *Excellent:* Students can access Internet-connected devices from any location with all-campus wireless networking for anytime, anywhere learning. Students are encouraged to use mobile devices for research and communication, integrating technology further into the curriculum instead of separating and banning its use.

1 = *Adequate:* Students can access Internet-connected computers during most of the day, but mobile devices are not supported.

0 = *Inadequate:* Technology is limited to centralized and static computer labs or computers at the back of the classroom. There is little or no connectivity, and mobile devices are not supported or allowed within the school.

Variety and flexibility of space: ☐

2 = *Excellent:* At least three types of spaces that support several learning modalities (e.g., small-group room, resource café area, and presentation area).

1 = *Adequate:* At least two types of spaces; a few opportunities for the students to change how the spaces look or are used.

0 = *Inadequate:* No variation in size and type of spaces (e.g., each classroom is the same size and is furnished for only one arrangement).

Lighting: ☐

2 = *Excellent:* Several types of lighting and the opportunity to vary it; easy ways to control levels of lighting (e.g., dimmers, shades); access to natural daylight.

1 = *Adequate:* No dimmers or other lighting controls, but a variety of lighting fixtures; some access to natural daylight.

0 = *Inadequate:* No opportunity to change the level of lighting; no variety in lighting; no access to natural daylight.

Furniture: ☐

2 = *Excellent:* A large variety of furniture and equipment that allows the students and teachers to change how the space looks and is used (e.g., move furnishings, create spaces, display their own work); furnishings are comfortable, are easy to use and move, and include soft seating.

1 = *Adequate:* Some variety of furniture and some areas are dedicated to flexible furniture arrangements, but not all.

0 = *Inadequate:* Little or no variation in the furniture, which is fixed and not adaptable to the different needs of the user.

Principal learning areas: ☐

2 = *Excellent:* The principal learning area allows for a variety of activities and includes a space for experimentation or messy work with adjacent cleanup facilities. Students have access to electronic and printed resources and project materials as well as prep and storage areas adjacent to work areas. There is ample space for all students and teachers to move around without congestion or awkward circulation.

1 = *Adequate:* There are cleanup facilities available only in specialized rooms, and the storage and prep areas are available to students during certain classes when they can be supervised. There is adequate space for almost all students to work actively and move around the room.

0 = *Inadequate:* There is little to no student access to resources and materials, and the storage areas are only for use by teachers. Cleanup facilities are not adjacent to project work areas. The space is limited and is problematic during active project working times.

Health and fitness: ☐

2 = *Excellent:* There are dedicated indoor and outdoor areas available for all students to use daily for play, exercise, and sports (e.g., yoga, dance, and aerobics studios; weight-lifting rooms; walking tracks). Also, accessibility to culinary health learning is included in the holistic view of the health and fitness education support system of the school (e.g., commercial kitchen facility open for students to learn healthy cooking; a fresh-food provider; student kitchenette available during the school day).

1 = *Adequate:* There is an indoor space that can be made available for exercise activities during certain hours of the day. There is a kitchenette available to students to bring and prepare their own food, or there is fresh-food provider.

0 = *Inadequate:* There are not adequate spaces for indoor exercise activities. If there is a kitchen, it is inaccessible to students, and there are no opportunities for culinary classes or for students to prepare their own food.

Restorative spaces: ☐

To combat cognitive fatigue, students and teachers need opportunities to engage in activities that do not require focused attention. Spaces for these restorative activities, such as watching birds at a feeder or leaves moving in the wind, should be accessible, where students can go on their own without needing to ask permission. Restorative spaces should contain items (e.g., soft furnishings, pillows, plants, a window seat, an aquarium) that are easy to access or view.

2 = *Excellent:* Three or more restorative spaces in the principal learning area.

1 = *Adequate:* One or two restorative spaces.

0 = *Inadequate:* No restorative spaces available.

Teachers as professionals: ☐

2 = *Excellent:* Teachers' workspaces are clustered together in small teams sharing a professional workroom with computers, phones, and other equipment. This space provides both formal and informal meeting spaces and is equipped with tools for collaborating and planning. The workroom is adjacent to principal learning areas and allows for passive supervision of the learning community.

1 = *Adequate:* Teachers share a semiprivate office. There is a common teacher workroom with necessary equipment accessible, but there is limited opportunity for informal and formal meeting and planning.

0 = *Inadequate:* Each teacher is isolated in his or her own classroom, with limited connections to other teachers for collaborating, planning, and socializing.

Informal learning areas: ☐

Spaces for students to gather (e.g., for eating, socializing, and collaborating) could have soft furnishings, café tables, benches, gathering stairs, etc., and should be visible and accessible to students.

2 = *Excellent:* Enough dedicated space and furniture for four or more students to gather, in more than three locations within the principal learning area.

1 = *Adequate:* Enough space and furniture for two or three students to gather, in at least two locations.

0 = *Inadequate:* No opportunities for students to gather and participate in informal learning activities.

Ethos, aesthetics, and community connection: ☐

2 = *Excellent:* The overall design and aesthetics of the school is responsive to the cultural ethos and context of the community. The entrance is welcoming, and there are several connections to the natural environment through windows, skylights, and outdoor learning spaces.

1 = *Adequate:* The entrance is welcoming, and there is some connection to the surrounding environment, but the scale and style of the school is not connected to the community.

0 = *Inadequate:* The design is not responsive to the community ethos, and there is little or no natural connection.

Score Card

Add up the scores for each category: ☐

20–28 = *Excellent:* High effectiveness in supporting twenty-first-century learning.

10–19 = *Adequate:* Acceptable performance in supporting twenty-first-century learning, but there is room for improvement.

0–10 = *Inadequate:* An urgent need for change to support twenty-first-century learning.

Source: Adapted from the classroom rating scale in Lorraine Maxwell, "Competency in Child Care Settings: The Role of the Physical Environment," *Environment and Behavior* 20, no. 10 (2006); and the EFEI (Educational Facilities Effectiveness Instrument), by FNI. © Fielding Nair International.

Notes

INTRODUCTION

1. My estimate is based on the following assumptions: the United States has a total of about 76 million students. Assuming a national average of about 130 square feet per student and a national average construction cost of $150 per square foot, the "value" of the built school facilities infrastructure is about $1.5 trillion. Assuming an additional 30 percent for other facilities-related investments such as land and play fields brings this total to approximately $2 trillion.

2. Paul Abramson, "17th Annual School Construction Report," *School Planning and Management*, February 2012, http://schoolplanning.epubxp.com/i/74777.

3. Diana G. Oblinger "Space as a Change Agent," in *Learning Spaces*, ed. Diana G. Oblinger (Boulder, CO: Educause, 2006), 8–10, cited in Stern Neill and R. Etheridge, "Flexible Learning Spaces: The Integration of Pedagogy, Physical Design, and Instructional Technology," *Marketing Education Review* 18, no. 1 (2008): 47–53.

4. Alfie Kohn, *The Schools Our Children Deserve: Moving Beyond Traditional Classrooms and "Tougher Standards"* (Boston: Houghton Mifflin, 1999).

5. *BusinessDictionary.com*, s.v. "Taylorism," accessed January 21, 2014, www.businessdictionary.com/definition/Taylorism.html.

6. David Warlick, web page, accessed January 21, 2014, www.davidwarlick.com.

7. Kohn, *The Schools Our Children Deserve*.

8. John Dewey, *Democracy and Education* (New York: Macmillan, 1916); Leslie Smith, "Jean Piaget, 1896–1980," in *Fifty Modern Thinkers on Education: From Piaget to the Present*, ed. Liora Bresler, David Cooper, and Joy Palmer (London: Routledge, 2001), 37–43.

9. Claudia Goldin and Lawrence Katz, *The Race Between Education and Technology* (Cambridge, MA: Belknap Press, 2008).

10. Richard Gerver, *Creating Tomorrow's Schools Today: Education—Our Children—Their Futures* (New York and London: Continuum International Publishing Group, 2010); Lisa Murphy, Emmanuel Mufti, and Derek Kassem, *Education Studies: An Introduction* (Berkshire, England: Open University Press, 2009).

11. Alfie Kohn, "Progressive Education: Why It's Hard to Beat, but Also Hard to Find," *Independent School* (spring 2008), www.alfiekohn.org/teaching/progressive.htm.

12. Peter Lippman, *Evidence-Based Design of Elementary and Secondary Schools* (Hoboken, NJ: John Wiley & Sons, 2010), 319.

13. *Wikipedia*, s.v. "one-room school," last modified January 7, 2014, http://en.wikipedia .org/wiki/One-room_school.

14. Frederick W. Taylor, *Scientific Management: Comprising Shop Management, the Principles of Scientific Management and Testimony Before the Special House Committee* (Westport, CT: Greenwood Publishing Group, 1972).

15. Virginia Heffernan, "Education Needs a Digital-Age Upgrade," *Opinionator*, blog of *New York Times*, August 7, 2011, http://opinionator.blogs.nytimes.com/2011/08/07/ education-needs-a-digital-age-upgrade/.

16. Kohn, *The Schools Our Children Deserve*.

17. Jeff Lackney, *Educational Facilities: The Impact and Role of the Physical Environment of the School on Teaching, Learning and Educational Outcomes*, Report R94-4 (Milwaukee: School of Architecture and Urban Planning, University of Wisconsin–Milwaukee, 1994), cited in Elliot Washor, *Innovative Pedagogy and School Facilities* (Minneapolis: Design Share, 2003), www.designshare.com/Research/Washor/Pedagogy%20and%20Facilities.pdf.

18. Larry Cuban, "Whatever Happened to the Open Classroom?" *Education Next* 4, no. 2 (2004), http://educationnext.org/files/ednext20042_68.pdf.

19. Bob Lingard and Martin Mills, "Teachers and School Reform: Working with Productive Pedagogies and Productive Assessment," *Melbourne Studies in Education* 44, no. 2 (2003): 1–18.

20. Ibid.; M. H. Bray, "Leading in Learning: An Analysis of Teachers' Interactions with Their Colleagues as They Implement a Constructivist Approach to Learning" (PhD diss., Vanderbilt University, Peabody College, Nashville, TN, 1998); Joan E. Talbert and Milbrey W. McLaughlin, "Understanding Teaching in Context," in *Teaching for Understanding: Challenges for Policy and Practice*, ed. David K. Cohen, Milbrey W. McLaughlin, and Joan E. Talbert (San Francisco: Jossey-Bass, 1993), 167–206.

21. Carrie R. Leana, "The Missing Link in School Reform," *Stanford Social Innovation Review* 9, no. 4 (2011), www.ssireview.org/articles/entry/the_missing_link_in_school_reform.

22. Robert S. Barth, "School as a Community of Leaders," in *Building a Professional Culture in Schools*, ed. A. Lieberman (New York: Teachers College Press, 1988), put it this way: "The relationship among adults who live in a school has more to do with the character and quality of the school *and* with the accomplishments of the students than any other factor."

23. National School Climate Center, "About Us," accessed January 21, 2014, http:// schoolclimate.org/about/.

24. J. A. Durlak et al., "The Impact of Enhancing Students' Social and Emotional Learning: A Meta-analysis of School-Based Universal Interventions," *Child Development* 82, no. 1 (2011): 405–432. A condensed version of this source is available at J. A. Durlak, "Study: Promoting Students' Personal and Social Development Boosts Academic Outcomes,

a Guest Blog by Joseph Durlak," *Edutopia* blog, March 23, 2011, www.edutopia.org/blog/social-emotional-learning-learning-boosts-academic-outcomes-joseph-durlak.

25. According to Ministry of Education Singapore, "Social and Emotional Learning," accessed January 21, 2014, www.moe.gov.sg/education/programmes/social-emotional-learning/, "the school environment is an important enabler of student learning that supports the teaching and learning of Social Emotional competencies."

26. Scott McLeod, "Teaching and Learning in the Era of Disruptive Innovation," PowerPoint presentation, accessed January 21, 2014, scottmcleod.org/2009NEAMcLeod.pptx.

27. Sylvia Libow Martinez and Gary Stager, *Invent to Learn: Making, Tinkering and Engineering in the Classroom* (Torrance, CA: Constructing Modern Knowledge Press, 2013).

28. David Orr, "What Is Education For?" The Learning Revolution series, *In Context* 27 (winter 1991), http://www.context.org/iclib/ic27/orr/.

29. Prakash Nair, "Getting Beyond School as Temple: What Do We Expect from Our Schools?" *Edutopia*, October 18, 2006, www.edutopia.org/getting-beyond-school-temple.

30. Mark Schneider, "Do School Facilities Affect Academic Outcomes?" National Clearinghouse for Educational Facilities, Washington, DC, November 2002, www.ncef.org/pubs/outcomes.pdf; Kenneth Tanner, "School Facilities: Physical Conditions in School Districts Receiving Impact Aid for Students Residing on Indian Lands," Report by US Government Accountability Office to the Chairman of the Committee on Indian Affairs US Senate, October 29, 2009, www.gao.gov/new.items/d1032.pdf.

31. Lorraine Maxwell, "Competency in Child Care Settings: The Role of the Physical Environment," *Environment and Behavior* 39, no. 2 (2007): 229–245; Fielding Nair International, "Education Facilities Effectiveness Instrument," accessed January 21, 2014, www.goodschooldesign.com/Default.aspx.

CHAPTER 1

1. The categories and descriptions used in this chapter are borrowed from two environmental rating scales in Fielding Nair International, "Education Facilities Effectiveness Instrument," accessed January 21, 2014, www.goodschooldesign.com/Default.aspx; Lorraine Maxwell, "Competency in Child Care Settings: The Role of the Physical Environment," *Environment and Behavior* 39, no. 2 (2007): 229–245; Lorraine Maxwell and Emily Chmielewski, "Environmental Personalization and Elementary School Children's Self-Esteem," *Journal of Environmental Psychology* 28, no. 2 (2008): 143–153.

2. Maxwell, "Competency in Child Care Settings."

3. Kenn Fisher, "Research into Identifying Effective Learning Environments," *Evaluating Quality in Educational Facilities* (2005), www.oecd.org/dataoecd/26/7/37905387.pdf.

4. Maxwell and Chmielewski, "Environmental Personalization and Elementary School Children's Self-Esteem"; Herb Childress, *Landscapes of Betrayal, Landscapes of Joy: Curtisville in the Lives of Its Teenagers* (Albany: State University of New York Press, 2000).

5. Steve Higgins et al., "The Impact of School Environments: A Literature Review," produced for the Design Council by The Centre for Learning and Teaching School of Education, Communication and Language Science at the University of Newcastle, 2005, www.ncl.ac.uk/cflat/about/documents/designcouncilreport.pdf.

6. Sue Allen, "Designs for learning: Studying Science Museum Exhibits That Do More Than Entertain," *Science Education* 88, no. S1 (2004): S17–S33.

7. James H. Banning, "Student Development: In-Between Buildings," *Journal of Student Affairs* 11 (2002): 21–25; R. Oldenburg, *Celebrating the Third Place* (New York: Marlowe & Company, 2001); James H. Banning, Stephanie Clemons, David McKelfresh, and Richard W. Gibbs, "Special Places for Students: Third Place and Restorative Place," *College Student Journal* 44, no. 4 (2010): 906–912.

8. Maria Klatte, Jürgen Hellbrück, Jochen Seidel, and Phillip Leistner, "Effects of Classroom Acoustics on Performance and Well-Being in Elementary School Children: A Field Study," *Environment and Behavior* 42, no. 5 (2010): 659–692, http://eab.sagepub.com/content/42/5/659.abstract.

9. Gary W. Siebein, Martin A. Gold, Glenn W. Siebein, and Michael G. Ermann, "Ten Ways to Provide a High-Quality Acoustical Environment in Schools," *Language, Speech and Hearing Services in Schools* 31 (October 2000): 381, www.siebeinacoustic.com/publications/journals/2000%20-%20Ten%20Ways%20to%20Provide%20a%20High-Quality%20Acoustical%20Env%20in%20Schools.pdf.

10. Gary W. Siebein et al., "Classroom Acoustics I: The Acoustical Learning Environment: Participatory Action Research in Classrooms," in *Proceedings of the International Congress on Acoustics*, ed. P. K. Kuhl and L. A. Crum (Seattle: Acoustical Society of America, 1998), 2721–2722, www.siebeinacoustic.com/publications/papers/1998%20-%20Classroom%20Acoustics%20I.pdf; Siebein, Gold, Siebein, and Ermann, "High-Quality Acoustical Environment," 381.

11. Banning, "Student Development: In-Between Buildings."

12. Maxwell, "Competency in Child Care Settings"; Rachel Kaplan, Stephen Kaplan, and Robert Ryan, *With People in Mind: Design and Management of Everyday Nature* (Washington, DC: Island Press, 1998).

13. Banning, Clemons, McKelfresh and Gibbs, "Special Places for Students."

14. Stephen Kaplan, "The Restorative Benefits of Nature: Toward an Integrative Framework," *Journal of Environmental Psychology* 15 (1995): 173, www.uns.ethz.ch/edu/teach/masters/ebcdm/readings/Kaplan_S.pdf.

15. F. L. Olmsted, *The Value and Care of Parks* (Reading, MA: Addison-Wesley, 1865), cited in *The American Environment: Readings in the History of Conservation*, ed. R. Nash (Reading, MA: Addison-Wesley), 18–24, cited in ibid., 174.

16. Fielding Nair International, "High School for Recording Arts," accessed January 22, 2014, www.fieldingnair.com/Projects/ProjectImages/Bigpopup.asp?fb=hsra_fb&pg=5.

17. Tim Rudd, Carolyn Gifford, Jo Morrison, and Keri Facer, "What If . . . : Re-Imagining Learning Spaces," Opening Education series, Futurelab, Bristol, UK, 2006, www.academia.edu/735528/Futurelab_What_if..._Re-imagining_learning_spaces.

18. Roine Leiringer and Paula Cardello, "Schools for the Twenty-First Century: School Design and Educational Transformation," *British Educational Research Journal* 37, no. 6 (2011): 915–934.

19. Rudd, Gifford, Morrison, and Facer, "What If . . . : Re-Imagining Learning Spaces."

20. Leigh Stringer, "Workplace Strategies That Enhance Performance, Health and Wellness," HOK Architects website, 2013, www.hok.com/thought-leadership/workplace-strategies-that-enhance-human-performance-health-and-wellness.

21. *Wikipedia*, s.v. "ergonomics," last modified May 18, 2013, http://en.wikipedia.org/wiki/Cognitive_ergonomics.

22. Peter Lippman, *Evidence-Based Design of Elementary and Secondary Schools* (Hoboken, NJ: John Wiley & Sons, 2010).

23. E. R. Sinofsky and F. G. Knirck, "Choose the Right Color for Your Learning Style," *Instructional Innovator* 26, no. 3 (1981): 17–19; A. H. Rice, "Color: What Research Knows About Color in the Classroom," *Nation's Schools* 1, no. 8 (1953), cited in Elizabeth Jago and Ken Tanner, "Influence of the School Facility on Student Achievement: Color," School Design and Planning Laboratory, University of Georgia, April 1999, www.coe.uga.edu/sdpl/researchabstracts/visual.html; S. P. Papadotas, "Color Them Motivated: Color's Psychological Effects on Students," *National Association of Secondary School Principals Bulletin* 57, no. 370 (1973): 92–94, cited in Jago and Tanner, "Influence of the School Facility on Student Achievement: Color"; Warren Hathaway, "Light, Colour, and Air Quality: Important Elements of the Learning Environment?" *Education Canada* 27, no. 3 (1987): 35–44, cited in Kathie Engelbrecht, "The Impact of Color on Learning," paper presented at NeoCon, Chicago, June 18, 2003, www.coe.uga.edu/sdpl/HTML/W305.pdf.

24. Engelbrecht, "The Impact of Color on Learning"; April Cottreau, "Colour Design for Better Classrooms," accessed January 22, 2014, http://catnet.adventist.ca/files/articles/pdf/tt_ID388.pdf; Heidi S. S. Johnson and Jennifer A. Maki, "Color Sense," *American School and University*, August 1, 2009, http://asumag.com/Construction/classroom-color-choices-200908/index.html; Ellen Kollie, "Light and Color Goes to School," *College Planning and Management*, June 2004, www.peterli.com/cpm/resources/articles/archive.php?article_id=842.

25. John Pile, *Color in Interior Design* (New York: McGraw Hill, 1997), 174–175.

26. Engelbrecht, "The Impact of Color on Learning."

27. Ibid.

28. Lorraine Maxwell, "Competency in Child Care Settings: The Role of the Physical Environment," *Environment and Behavior* 20, no. 10 (2006).

CHAPTER 2

1. Marc G. Berman, John Jonides, and Stephen Kaplan, "The Cognitive Benefits of Interacting with Nature," Department of Psychology, Department of Industrial and Operations Engineering, and Department of Electrical Engineering and Computer Science, University of Michigan, 2008. The researchers experimented with cognitive and executive functions after exposure to walking outside and found that functioning improved during a short nature walk, despite weather conditions or time of year.

2. Jing Wang, Ronald J. Iannotti, and Tonja R. Nansel, "School Bullying Among Adolescents in the United States: Physical, Verbal, Relational, and Cyber," National Institutes of Health, Bethesda, March 31, 2009.

3. Jane Jacobs, *The Death and Life of Great American Cities* (New York: Random House, 1961).

4. James H. Noonan and Malissa C. Vavra, "Crime in Schools and Colleges: A Study of Offenders and Arrestees Reported via National Incident-Based Reporting System Data," US Department of Justice, Federal Bureau of Investigation, October 2007, www.fbi.gov/about-us/cjis/ucr/nibrs/crime-in-schools-and-colleges-pdf.

5. Randall Fielding, "Learning, Lighting and Color: Lighting Design for Schools and Universities in the 21st Century," DesignShare.com, 2006, www.designshare.com/articles/1/133/fielding_light-learn-color.pdf.

6. Marie Louise Bistrup, ed., *Health Effects of Noise on Children* (Copenhagen: National Institute of Public Health, 2001), www.si-folkesundhed.dk/upload/health-effects-noise-children.pdf.

7. Bryan Lawson, *The Language of Space* (Woburn, MA: Reed Educational and Professional Publishing, 2001).

8. Therese Jilek, "A Variety of Voices: Innovative Learning Spaces Transform the Hartland-Lakeside School District, "DesignShare.com, http://www.designshare.com/index.php/a-variety-of-voices-innovative-learning-spaces-transform-the-hartland-lakeside-school-district/, May 31, 2012.

9. Ibid.

CHAPTER 3

1. Sonit Bafna et al., "Designing Space to Support Knowledge Work," *Environment and Behavior* 39, no. 6 (2007): 815–840; C. Carney Strange and James Banning, *Educating by Design: Creating Campus Learning Environments That Work* (San Francisco: Jossey-Bass, 2001); Mark Schneider, "Do Facilities Affect Academic Outcomes?" National Clearinghouse for Educational Facilities, November 2002, www.ncef.org/pubs/outcomes .pdf; Kenn Fisher, "Building Better Outcomes: The Impact of School Infrastructure on Student Outcomes and Behaviour," Department of Education, Training and Youth Affairs, Australia, 2001; Glen Earthman, "Prioritization of 31 Criteria for School Building Adequacy," American Civil Liberties Union Foundation of Maryland, Baltimore, January 5, 2004, www.schoolfunding.info/policy/facilities/ACLUfacilities_ report1-04.pdf; Kim Mickenberg. "A Room with a View," *Psychology Today* 41, no. 4 (2008): 51; David Pugsley and Barry Haynes, "An Alternative Use of Space in Government Office Accommodation," *Facilities* 20, nos. 1–2 (2002): 34–40; Mahlon Apgar IV, "The Alternative Workplace: Changing Where and How People Work," *Harvard Business Review* 76, no. 3 (1998); Andrew Morgan and Sarah Anthony, "Creating a High-Performance Workplace: A Review of Issues and Opportunities," *Journal of Corporate Real Estate* 10, no. 1 (2008): 27–39; Ardeshir Mahdavi and Ulla Unzeitig, "Occupancy Implications of Spatial, Indoor-Environmental, and Organizational Features of Office Spaces," *Building and Environment* 40, no. 1 (2005): 113–123; Adrian Leaman and Bill Bordass, "Productivity in Buildings: The 'Killer' Variables," *Building Research and Information* 27, no. 1 (1999): 4–19.

2. Ron A. Astor and Heather Ann Meyer, "Where Girls and Women Won't Go: Female Students', Teachers', and Social Workers' Views of School Safety," *Social Work in Education* 12, no. 4 (1999): 201–219; Jodi Lipson, ed., "Hostile Hallways: Bullying, Teasing and Sexual Harassment in School," American Association of University Women Educational Foundation, Washington, DC, 2001, http://www.aauw.org/files/2013/02/ hostile-hallways-bullying-teasing-and-sexual-harassment-in-school.pdf; Frieda D. Peatross and John Peponis, "Space, Education, and Socialization," *Journal of Architectural and Planning Research* 12, no.4 (1995): 366–385; Intervention Central, "Locations: Transforming Schools from Bully-Havens to Safe Havens," Intervention Central.org, accessed January 30, 2014, www.interventioncentral.org/behavioral-interventions/ bully-prevention/locations-transforming-schools-bully-havens-safe-havens.

3. David D. Thornburg, *Campfires in Cyberspace* (Lake Barrington, IL: Starsong, 1999); David D. Thornburg, "Campfires in Cyberspace: Primordial Metaphors for Learning in the Twenty-First Century," *Ed at a Distance Magazine* 15, no. 6 (2001), www.usdla .org/html/journal/JUN01_Issue/article01.html.

4. Prakash Nair and Annalise Gehling. "Places for Learning in the Twenty-First Century," *Education Matters: Primary and Secondary* 1 (2012): 90–94, http://ebook.aprs.com .au/issue/55912.

5. This section is largely excerpted from Randall Fielding and Prakash Nair, "Small Is Big: Breaking Down Schools to Break Down Barriers," *Edutopia*, October 24, 2005, www.edutopia.org/small-is-big-breaking-down-schools-to-break-down-barriers.

6. Kathleen Cotton, "New Small Learning Communities: Findings from Recent Literature," Northwest Regional Educational Laboratory, Portland, OR, December 2001, www.education.vermont.gov/new/pdfdoc/dept/transformation/commission/policy _development_resources/shared_accountability/educ_sa_new_small_learning_ communities.pdf.

7. Malcolm Gladwell, *The Tipping Point: How Little Things Can Make a Big Difference* (Boston: Little, Brown, 2000).

8. Aleks Krotoski, "Robin Dunbar: We Can Only Ever Have 150 Friends at Most . . . .," *The (London) Observer*, March 13, 2010, www.guardian.co.uk/technology/2010/ mar/14/my-bright-idea-robin-dunbar.

9. Tom Gregory, "Fear of Success? Ten Ways Alternative Schools Pull Their Punches," *The Phi Delta Kappan* 82, no. 8 (2001): 577–581.

CHAPTER 4

1. Katerina Ananiadou and Magdalean Claro, "21st Century Skills and Competences for New Millennium Learners in OECD Countries," Working Paper 41, Organisation for Economic Co-operation and Development, Education, OECD Publishing, December 18, 2009, http://dx.doi.org/10.1787/218525261154.

2. Assessment and Teaching of 21st Century Skills, "What Are 21st-Century Skills?" University of Melbourne, Australia, accessed January 21, 2014, http://atc21s.org/ index.php/about/what-are-21st-century-skills/; Partnership for 21st Century Skills, "Framework for 21st Century Learning," www.p21.org/our-work/p21-framework.

3. *Merriam-Webster.com*, s.v. "laboratory," accessed January 21, 2014, www.merriam-webster .com/dictionary/laboratory.

4. Susan R. Singer, Margaret L. Hilton, and Heidi A. Schweingruber, eds., for Board of Science Education and the Center for Education, National Research Council, *America's Lab Report: Investigations into High School Science* (Washington, DC: National Academies Press, 2006), www.nap.edu/openbook.php?record_id=11311&page=193.

5. Ibid.

6. Ibid.

7. Ibid.

8. Ibid.

9. David B. Zandvliet, *Education Is Not Rocket Science: The Case for Deconstructing Computer Labs* (Rotterdam: Sense Publishers, 2006).

10. Steve Minten and Stephen Seyfer, "Gibraltar Schools: One Laptop Per Student," handout, Annual Rural Schools Alliance Conference, Rothschild, WI, November 16–17, 2011, www.uwosh.edu/ruralschools/conference/documents/Gibraltrar_Schools_handout_2011.pdf.

11. Prakash Nair, Randall Fielding, and Jeffery Lackney "Master Classroom: Design Inspired by Creative Minds," *Edutopia*, October 18, 2006, www.edutopia.org/master-classroom.

12. Association for Science Education, "School Science Architecture Special Report Part Two: Science Lab Design," January 24, 2011, www.ase.org.uk/documents/science-labs-in-secondary-schools/.

13. Brit Morin, "What Is the Maker Moment and Why Should You Care?" *Huff Post Tech*, blog of *Huffington Post*, October 4, 2013, www.huffingtonpost.com/brit-morin/what-is-the-maker-movemen_b_3201977.html.

14. TechShop is a "vibrant, creative community that provides access to tools, software and space" (TechShop home page, accessed January 30, 2014, www.techshop.ws/).

15. Sylvia Libow Martinez and Gary Stager, *Invent to Learn: Making, Tinkering and Engineering in the Classroom* (Torrance, CA: Constructing Modern Knowledge Press, Torrance, CA, 2013).

CHAPTER 5

1. Y. L. Goddard, R. D. Goddard, and M. Tschannen-Moran, "A Theoretical and Empirical Investigation of Teacher Collaboration for School Improvement and Student Achievement in Public Elementary Schools," *Teachers College Record* 109, no. 4 (2007): 877–896; C. M. Guarino, L. Santibanez, and G. A. Daley, "Teacher Recruitment and Retention: A Review of the Recent Empirical Literature," *Review of Educational Research* 76, no. 2 (2006): 173–208; and S. M. Kardos and S. M. Johnson, "On Their Own and Presumed Expert: New Teachers' Experience with Their Colleagues," *Teachers College Record* 109, no. 9 (2007): 2,083–2,106, www.cstp-wa.org/Navigational/Policies_practices/Teacher_induction/KardosNewTeachersandCulture.pdf.

2. Carrie R. Leana, "The Missing Link in School Reform," *Stanford Social Innovation Review* (fall 2011), www.ssireview.org/articles/entry/the_missing_link_in_school_reform/.

CHAPTER 6

1. Susan La Marca, ed., (2007) *Rethink: Ideas for Inspiring School Library Design* (Melbourne, Australia: School Libraries Association of Victoria, 2007).

2. Jennifer LaGarde, "The Future of Libraries Is Now," in *School Libraries: What's Now, What's Next, What Comes After*, ed. by Kristin Fontichiaro and Buffy Hamilton (e-book, published by Kristin Fontichiaro and Buffy Hamilton on Smashwords, 2011).

3. Evantheia Schibsted, "Way Beyond Fuddy-Duddy: New Libraries Bring Out the Best in Students," *Edutopia*, September 26, 2005, www.edutopia.org/school-library-design.

CHAPTER 7

1. Richard Louv, *Last Child in the Woods: Saving Our Children from Nature-Deficit Disorder* (Chapel Hill, NC: Algonquin Books, 2005), quoted in Timothy Egan, "Nature-Deficit Disorder," *Opinionator*, blog of *New York Times*, March 29, 2012, http://opinionator.blogs.nytimes.com/2012/03/29/nature-deficit-disorder/.

2. Rachel Kaplan and Stephen Kaplan, *The Experience of Nature: A Psychological Perspective* (Cambridge and New York: Cambridge University Press, 1989).

3. Tara Parker-Pope, "Natural Settings Help Brain Fatigue," *Opinionator*, blog of *New York Times*, October 27, 2008, http://well.blogs.nytimes.com/2008/10/27/natural-settings-help-brain-fatigue.

4. A. F. Taylor, F. E. Kuo, and W. C. Sullivan, "Coping with ADD: The Surprising Connection to Green Play Settings," *Environment and Behavior* 33, no. 1 (2001): 54–77.

5. Karen Malone and Paul Tranter, "Children's Environmental Learning and the Use, Design and Management of Schoolgrounds," *Children, Youth and Environments* 13, no. 2 (2003).

6. William Crain, "Now Nature Helps Children Develop," *Montessori Life* (summer 2001).

7. E. Cobb, *The Ecology of Imagination in Childhood* (New York: Columbia University Press, 1977); Richard Louv, *Childhood's Future* (New York: Doubleday, 1991).

8. Ruth A. Wilson, "The Wonders of Nature: Honoring Children's Ways of Knowing," *Early Childhood News* 6, no. 19 (1997).

9. Robin Moore, "Compact Nature: The Role of Playing and Learning Gardens on Children's Lives," *Journal of Therapeutic Horticulture* 8 (1996): 72–82.

10. R. Nowak, "Blame Lifestyle for Myopia, Not Genes," *NewScientist*, July 10, 2004, 12.

11. Sheridan Bartlett, "Access to Outdoor Play and Its Implications for Healthy Attachments," unpublished article, Putney, VT, 1996.

12. Moore, "Compact Nature."

13. Prakash Nair, Randall Fielding, and Jeff Lackney, *The Language of School Design*, 2nd ed. (Minneapolis: DesignShare, 2009).

14. Miki Perkins, "Hey Adults, We Just Want to Let Our Hair Down," *The Age (Melbourne, Australia)*, June 9, 2012, .

CHAPTER 8

1. On the links between a poor school environment and student vandalism, see Susan Black, "The Roots of Vandalism," *American School Board Journal* 189, no. 7 (2002): 30–32. On the general importance of school design, see Steve Higgins et al., "The Impact of School Environments: A Literature Review," Design Council, University of Newcastle, Newcastle upon Tyne, UK, February 2005, www.ncl.ac.uk/cflat/news/DCReport.pdf.

2. Stephanie Alexander, *Kitchen Garden Cooking with Kids* (Melbourne, Australia: Penguin Lantern, 2006).

CONCLUSION

1. Lorraine Maxwell, "Competency in Child Care Settings: The Role of the Physical Environment," *Environment and Behavior* 39, no. 2 (2007): 229–245; Fielding Nair International, "Education Facilities Effectiveness Instrument," accessed January 21, 2014, www.goodschooldesign.com/Default.aspx.

ACKNOWLEDGMENTS

As with most meaningful achievements in life, this one was by no means a one-man show. Featured here are the key behind-the-scenes people whose combined brilliance made this book possible and to all of whom I extend my sincerest thank you. To my wife Jody Sampson-Nair, whose love and profound influence on my life is evidenced in all that I do—every page in this book carries her imprint; to my children Delta, Mallika, and Jake, who give meaning and purpose to my life in too many ways to fully describe here; to my "bro" and business partner Randy Fielding, whose magic touch as a world-renowned architect is visible throughout this book in the many projects featured here. To my mother and father and my brother Deepak for an enchanted childhood and too many reasons to list individually.

To Gayle Johnson, whose valued friendship and wise counsel I depended upon time and again during the course of developing the ideas found within these pages. To Cathy Roberts-Martin, who worked closely with me on all the chapters, provided invaluable design and logistical help, and was particularly instrumental in developing the chapter on welcoming entries. To Annalise Gehling, whose expert help as an innovative educator was critical in shaping the chapters on teachers' areas, cafés, libraries, and the outdoors. To Kelli Ogboke, who contributed to the labs chapter and also helped me immensely with the extensive research that went into the writing of this book.

I had almost given up trying to find someone to illustrate the book after a futile Internet search when I discovered Kristie Anderson in our Washington, D.C., studio—her beautiful work adorns most of the chapters in this book.

To each of my friends, professional colleagues, and extended family at Fielding Nair International—Jay Litman, Isaac Williams, James Seaman, Jennifer Lamar, Rits Marcelis, Danielle McCarthy, Louis Sirota, Travis Pennock, Chris Hazleton, Melvin Freestone, Kris Fielding, Sally Zesbaugh, Michael Van Hamel, Mike Bykovski, Michael Fischer, Bipin Bhadran, Bob Pearlman, and Gary Stager, for the amazing schools they are helping to create—the source of so much of my inspiration.

To all the brave educators I have had the good fortune to work with and who spend most of every day being the strongest advocates they can be for children. Among them, Bruce Rockstroh, Kevin Bartlett, Amy Wasser, Rosemarie Kraeger, Rob Glass, Craig Johnson, Joe Atherton, Steve Freedman, Lynda Hayes, Mike Murphy, Paul Turnbull, Lyn McKay, Robert Rhodes, and Brett Jacobsen deserve special mention.

Last but most definitely not the least, to my editor Caroline Chauncey, who proposed the idea for this book and then spent many countless hours helping me flesh out and refine each chapter. Without her initiative, direction, and encouragement, this book would not have been written.

About the Author

PRAKASH NAIR is the president of Fielding Nair International (FNI), a renowned international architectural firm that specializes in the design of innovative schools. FNI has consultations in forty-three countries on six continents. Prakash is a futurist, a visionary planner, an architect, and one of the world's leading change agents in education and school design. He has helped dozens of communities globally to align their physical space with their pedagogical needs. He is the recipient of several international awards, including the prestigious CEFPI MacConnell Award, the top honor worldwide for school design.

He has written extensively in leading national and international journals. His work has been published in *Education Week*, *School Planning and Management* magazine, *School Business Affairs*, *School Construction News*, *Edutopia*, Annenberg Institute's *VUE*, OECD's *Programme on Educational Building*, the United Kingdom's *Schools for Life*, Australian Education Union's *Professional Voice*, *Teacher: The National Education Magazine* of Australia, and *Rethink!—Ideas for Inspiring School Library Design*. He also coauthored, with Randall Fielding, the landmark publication *The Language of School Design*.

He has been interviewed many times by print, radio, and television media and is a regular speaker and keynote presenter at international education conferences. You can learn more about Prakash Nair and the projects featured in this book by visiting http://FieldingNair.com, or contact him at Prakash@FieldingNair.com.

Index

academic achievement, 13
achievement gap, 5
acoustics, 34–35, 52
activities matrix, 63
administration offices, 50–51
advisory model, 37–38, 76
aesthetics, 43
agility, 19–20, 58, 79
air quality, 32
alternative spaces, 94–103
amphitheaters, 142, 144
antisocial behavior, 14
architects, 163–164
assembly lines, 2, 8
assessment, of existing spaces, 161–162
attention deficit/hyperactivity disorder
    (ADHD), 130, 131
attention restoration theory, 36, 129–130

bathrooms, 36
BiblioTech, 124
black-box theater, 101–103
Bloomfield Hills High School, 170–171
bookless libraries, 124
bullying, 14, 36, 49, 51
bus areas, 46

cafés, 148, 150–154
cafeterias
    acoustics in, 35
    features of welcoming, 146
    furnishings for, 147–148, 150–151
    gardens and, 155, 157, 158
    positive behaviors in, 157
    redesigning, 145–157
    student involvement in running of, 155–157
    students and teachers sharing, 112
    support for student learning activities in,
        153–157
    tips for improving, 149
    versatility in, 147–153
    welcoming students into, 146–147
cafetoriums, 18–19, 147
campfire metaphor, 64, 66, 67, 87, 101
carpet, 34, 43
case studies, 164–171
cave metaphor, 64, 66, 67, 87
cells-and-bells model, 2, 61, 90
chairs, 40, 41
classrooms
    acoustics in, 34
    cells-and-bells model, 2, 61, 90
    learning modalities and, 67–70, 81–82
    as learning studios, 62, 63, 69, 70–73
    as learning suites, 73
    libraries in, 121–122
    low-cost renovations for, 63
    reconfiguring, 61–80
    as single-purpose spaces, 64
    as small learning communities, 73–80
class sets, of equipment, 91
clutter, 43, 44
cognitive ergonomics, 40
cognitive fatigue, 130

collaborative environment, 13
college graduates, 5
color rendition index (CRI), 33
colors, 42
common spaces, 51–58
community
    connection to, 16
    entrances and, 49
    identity, 43
    school commons and, 55–56
    small learning communities (SLCs), 73–80
community commons, 55–58
community libraries, 125–126
compulsory schooling, 6–8
computer labs, 92–94
computers, 38–39

David Thompson Secondary School, 156
Da Vinci studio, 94–96
daylight, 33–34, 42, 43
departmental groupings, of teachers, 108
design principles, 11–16, 26–27, 78–80, 145–146
digital libraries, 124
digital literacy, 14
discovery process, 162–163
displays, 54
distributed technology, 89

early-childhood classrooms, 70
education
    design for, 11–16
    history of U.S., 6–11
educational commissioning, 103
educational model
    factory-based, 7–9, 16, 90
    skills-based, 84–85
    student-centered, 1–6, 8–10, 12, 109
    teacher-centered, 2–4, 10, 109
    traditional, 2

electronic media, 119–120, 124
electronic monitoring, 50
eletronic displays, 54
entrances, 45–54, 59–60
environment
        See also nature
    connection to, 15
    learning buildings and the, 19–20
ergonomic chairs, 40, 41
espresso studio, 96–97
ethos, 43
experiential learning, 136–141
experimental theater, 101–103
"eyes on the street", 50

facilities master plan, 162
facilities planner, 163–164
factory-model schools, 7–9, 16, 90
fieldwork, 134, 136–141
flexibility, 19, 29–31
flexible scheduling, 15, 134
floor sufaces, 43
fluorescent light, 33
Fordist model, 8
Forest Avenue Elementary School, 164–165, 168
forest school movement, 137–138
furnishings, 40–42, 52–53, 63, 92, 147–148, 150–151

gang violence, 49
gardens, 99, 101, 155, 157, 158
glare, 34
global network, connection to, 16
Glodin, Claudia, 5
Google, 118
greenery, 140
green technologies, 17
gymnatoriums, 18–19, 147

hallways
    reconfiguring, 61–62, 65
    as single-purpose spaces, 64
hands-on learning, 83, 85, 87, 90, 136–141
heart of school, 51–54
Hillel Academy, 165–166, 167, 168
home base, 37–38
Horace Greeley High School, 166–167, 169–170
human capital, 13
human development, nature and, 129–132
human observation, 50

incremental change, 159–161
industry partnerships, 91
informal learning areas, 31–32
information access, 116–117
inside goes outside, 134, 141–144
integrated learning areas, 83–103
interdisciplinary approach, 99
interior design, 39–43
Internet, 89, 117–118

Jamie Oliver studio, 99–101

Katz, Lawrence, 5
kitchen gardens, 99, 101, 155, 157, 158
kivas, 86

labor market, 5
lab spaces
    computer labs, 92–94
    cost-effective, 91
    Da Vinci studio, 94–96
    essential qualities of good, 85
    furnishings for, 92
    maker lab, 98–99
    rethinking, 84–88

science labs, 88–92
landscaping, 46–47
laptops, 38
leadership team, 162–163
learning
    modalities, 67–70, 81–82, 134–144
    multiple ways of, 67–70
learning areas
    alternative spaces, 94–103
    informal, 31–32
    integrated, 83–103
    multi-purpose spaces, 18–19, 29–31,
        83–103
    outdoor, 48, 129–144
learning building, concept of, 6, 16–20
learning communities, 15, 151
    acoustics and, 34–35
    entries to, 58
learning environment, 32–35
learning metaphors, 64–67, 87, 101
learning studios, 62, 63, 69, 70–73, 77
learning suites, 62, 73
learning terraces, 142, 143, 144
LED lighting, 33
libraries. *See* school libraries
life learning principles, 87–88
life metaphor, 64, 66, 67, 87, 99, 101
lighting, 33–34, 52
low-cost renovations, 63

maintenance expenses, 1
maker lab, 98–99
maker movement, 14, 98
mass manufacturing, 8
materials, 42–43
media resource centers (MRCs), 120–123
    See also school libraries
mental fatigue, 36
Middletown Public Schools, 164–165, 168
monotone environments, 42

Montessori, Maria, 8
multidisciplinary approach, 91, 92
multiple learning centers, 12
multi-purpose spaces, 18–19, 29–31, 83–
    103

National School Climate Center, 13
natural light, 52
nature
    educational strategies and, 132, 134
    importance of, 129–132
network model, 16
nooks, 36, 122

one-room schoolhouses, 6–7
open-classrooms movement, 8, 9–11
Orr, David W., 15
outdoor areas, 48, 129–144

partitions, 76, 77
passive supervision, 50–51
pedagogy, 161
personalization, 35–38
personalized learning, 4
pilot projects, 159–160
play spaces, 134, 135–136, 137
positive school climate, 12–14, 51–54, 79–80,
    134
primary colors, 42
primordial learning metaphors, 64–67, 87,
    101
print media, 120
privacy, 35–36
professional design team, 163–164
professional development, 13, 103, 161
progressive education movement, 5
project-based learning, 4, 15, 85, 87, 90
Prussian movement, 7

reciprocity, in learning, 6
renovations, low-cost, 63
restorative areas, 36

safety, at entrances, 49–51
satellite libraries, 120–123
scale, 29
scheduling, 15, 134
school buildings
    assessment of existing spaces in, 161–162
    average age of, 1
    as community resources, 55–56
    design principles for, 11–16, 26–27, 78–80,
        145–146
    entrances to, 45–54, 59–60
    incremental change for, 159–161
    influence of, 16–18, 25
    money invested in, 1, 2, 17
    open-classrooms movement and, 9–11
    scale of, 29
    smart, 19
    traditional, 1–3, 8
    visual cues of, 26
school bus areas, 46
school cafeterias. *See* cafeterias
school climate, positive, 12–14, 51–54, 79–80,
    134
school commons, 55–58
school day, 15
school design
    agile, 19, 58, 79
    cafeterias, 145–157
    case studies, 164–171
    classrooms, 61–80
    for education, 11–16
    elements of good, 27–44
    history of, 6–11
    innovation in, 8–9
    for outdoor learning, 129–144
    putting theory into practice, 159–173

for small learning communities, 75–80
for teacher collaboration, 105–114
technology and, 11, 38–39
traditional, 1–3, 8
uniqueness in, 46
use of partitions in, 76, 77
school leadership team (SLT), 162–163
school libraries, 115–128
  bookless, 124
  community libraries and, 125–126
  features of good, 116
  future of, 126–128
  information access and, 116–117
  role of, 115–117
  satellite, 120–123
  teacher-librarians, 117–118
  transforming, 127
  underused, 123–125
  virtual, 119–120
school shootings, 49
schools without walls, 9
    See also open-classrooms movement
science labs, 88–92
search engines, 117–118
seating options, 30, 40, 41, 52–53, 63
security, at entrances, 49–51
signage, 46, 48, 53–54
signature elements, 46, 47, 48–49, 54
skills-based model, 84–85
small learning communities (SLCs), 72,
    73–80
small schools, 73–75
smartphones, 89
smart school buildings, 19
social areas, 49
social capital, 13
social discourse, 36
social-emotional learning, 4, 13
social media, 119–120
soft fascinations, 36, 130
spatial organization, 28–32

student-centered learning
  about, 4–6
  design for, 12
  movement for, 8–10
  nature and, 134
  shifting to, 109
  traditional school design and, 1–3
student displays, 54
students
  agile, 19–20
  personal spaces for, 35–38
  ratio between teachers and, 72
  in teacher-centered education, 2, 3–4
studios
  Da Vinci studio, 94–96
  espresso studio, 96–97
  Jamie Oliver studio, 99–101
sunlight, 33–34

tablets, 89
tack boards, 42–43
Taylor, Frederick, 2
Taylorism, 2, 8, 16
teacher-centered learning, 2–4, 10, 109
teacher collaboration, 13, 105–114, 134
teacher-librarians, 117–118
teacher offices, 105–112
teachers' lounge, 112–114
teacher-student ratio, 72
teaching methods, 161
technology
  distributed, 89
  electronic displays, 54
  green, 17
  integration of, 14–15, 134
  role of, in education, 11
  use of, 38–39
textures, 42–43
thermal comfort, 32
third place, 31–32

traditional school design, 1–3, 8
twenty-first-century schools, cost of, 17

urban settings, outdoor learning in,
        133

vandalism, 37
variety, 29–31
versatility, 12, 79, 147–153
violence, 49
virtual libraries, 119–120

visual literacy
    defined, 25
    design elements for, 27–44
    school buildings and, 26

walkways, 46–47
watering hole metaphor, 64, 66, 67, 87, 99, 101
welcoming environment, 12, 79
whiteboards, 38
wireless access, 39, 54
workspaces, teacher, 105–114
workstations, 37–38